Praise for Alicia Kennedy's *No Meat Required*

"Though not a traditional cookbook in any sense of the word, everyone who loves to cook is excited about *No Meat Required*, food writer Alicia Kennedy's contribution to the conversation about plant-based eating. In her signature evocative and thoughtful prose, Kennedy asks the reader to join her in questioning meat's role in our culture."

—*Vogue*

"One of the pleasures of reading this book is that it prompts us to think about nature's variety and abundance, and about how that abundance can show up on our plates."

—*The Atlantic*

"*No Meat Required* serves up a well-researched look at American veganism and lays the groundwork for plant-based cuisine."

—*Chicago Review of Books*

"*No Meat Required* was always going to be a hugely important book, but it didn't have to be a total pleasure. This is what happens when a writer as curious, compassionate, and truth-seeking as Kennedy goes all out on a subject that she knows matters deeply, to her and to the world."

—Lauren Collins, staff writer, *The New Yorker*

"In a dietary discourse starved for historical and cultural context, Alicia's work and analysis on the politics of eating meat (or not!) have been enduringly informed and insightful, punctuated by *No Meat Required*. There's no one else I'd rather read on the subject!"

—Stephen Satterfield, host of *High on the Hog* and founder of Whetstone Media

"Everyone, whether vegan, vegetarian, or omnivorous, needs to read this elegantly written, thought-provoking treatise."

—Nigella Lawson

"An impressively exhaustive look at where vegetable-centered eating comes from and where it might head, and a vital reminder that today's dominant idea of veganism tells very little of the story."

—Tamar Adler, author of *An Everlasting Meal*

ON EATING

Also by Alicia Kennedy

No Meat Required: The Cultural History and Culinary Future of Plant-Based Eating

ON EATING

The Making and Unmaking of My Appetites

ALICIA KENNEDY

New York Boston

This memoir reflects the author's life faithfully rendered to the best of her ability. Some names and identifying details have been changed to protect the privacy of others.

Copyright © 2026 by Alicia Kennedy

Jacket design by Dana Li. Jacket artwork "Oysters and Champagne" © Amelia Jayne Art Ltd. Jacket copyright © 2026 by Hachette Book Group, Inc.

Hachette Book Group supports the right to free expression and the value of copyright. The purpose of copyright is to encourage writers and artists to produce the creative works that enrich our culture.

The scanning, uploading, and distribution of this book without permission is a theft of the author's intellectual property. If you would like permission to use material from the book (other than for review purposes), please contact permissions@hbgusa.com. Thank you for your support of the author's rights.

Balance
Hachette Book Group
1290 Avenue of the Americas
New York, NY 10104
GCP-Balance.com
@GCPBalance

First Edition: April 2026

Balance is an imprint of Grand Central Publishing. The Balance name and logo are registered trademarks of Hachette Book Group, Inc.

The publisher is not responsible for websites (or their content) that are not owned by the publisher.

The Hachette Speakers Bureau provides a wide range of authors for speaking events. To find out more, go to hachettespeakersbureau.com or email HachetteSpeakers@hbgusa.com.

Balance books may be purchased in bulk for business, educational, or promotional use. For information, please contact your local bookseller or the Hachette Book Group Special Markets Department at special.markets@hbgusa.com.

Print book interior design by Amy Quinn

Library of Congress Cataloging-in-Publication Data

Names: Kennedy, Alicia (Food writer) author
Title: On eating : the making and unmaking of my appetites / Alicia Kennedy.
Description: First edition. | New York ; Boston : Balance, 2026. | Includes bibliographical references.
Identifiers: LCCN 2025049063 | ISBN 9780306836336 hardcover | ISBN 9780306836350 ebook
Subjects: LCSH: Kennedy, Alicia (Food writer) | Food | Cooking | Gastronomy
Classification: LCC TX649.K425 A3 2026
LC record available at https://lccn.loc.gov/2025049063

ISBNs: 9780306836336 (hardcover), 9780306836350 (ebook)

Printed in the United States of America

LSC-C

Printing 1, 2026

Contents

From Eater to Cook

As a girl, I ate like a king.

From my spot on a plastic toy peering through the railing from the living room down toward the front door, I heard my grandmother call to my grandfather when he walked in from work. "Go get lamb chops," she said, and he spun right back around to go to the Grand Union. In the replay of this first memory, a memory I've held close for my entire life, I see my grandpa, clad in a gray suit, close his eyes in exhaustion. But still, he did it without argument. I'm not sure why. I'll never know the intricacies of their relationship and what my constant presence in their house meant within it during those early years of my life. All I knew was that there was no debate: I wanted lamb chops; there would be lamb chops.

That was the power I had as a toddler, as the firstborn grandchild. What I wanted, I got, whether it was lamb chops for dinner or the latest cereal advertised on children's television. This appetite I was born with amused those around me; no one ever, to my knowledge, suggested it should be of concern. I ate whole lobsters, dipping their flesh in melted butter, while still in a high chair. You can't make up this kind of self-mythology for a food writer; it would seem over the top.

This is something I've been slow to admit, that I've got a unique relationship to food that's never been punishing. I feel too lucky; the luck feels embarrassing, considering the ways in which food can be burden, weapon, and misery for so many. It's been the opposite for me: pure elation, when I get to try a new tropical fruit, or there are fried artichokes on the menu, or I tell stories of how I'd delight in fried clam strips during Long Island summers, followed up by a cup of vanilla soft-serve in a tiny Yankees helmet at Carvel or a Ralph's Italian Ice in the flavor rainbow. What did a rainbow taste like? Like summer on the bay, just as deeply as those chewy, salty fried clam strips, their layer of breading softened by a squeeze of lemon. Or it tasted like fake cherry and fake lemon, but why ruin the mystique of trying to contain a rainbow in a flavored ice? Rainbow flavor is whatever you need it to be in that moment.

Did I become first a baker and then a food writer because my grandma instilled in me the importance of eating well? Or was it because I learned, eventually, that this would be a way of always finding my way back to her—to maybe the first and last relationship of my life that had no complications, no thorns? It was white sugar on strawberries: sweet on sweet, all the tartness drawn out into the juice I didn't drink. With my grandma, I had a home outside of my immediate family and its explosive emotions.

—

They say memories you often replay become memories of the memories, in which case I'm watching the tape of a tape of a tape of everything I can recall of my grandma, born Elizabeth Webb in 1932 and called Betty by those who knew her. The family lore varies on why my great-grandmother, known as Mum-Mum, turned away my great-grandfather, Wise Webb, one day, but Betty grew up in Bay Ridge, Brooklyn, as a daughter alone among many adults, and I like to believe it's because she refused to leave her Brooklyn for his Virginia. Why leave Brooklyn? Why leave New York? (I couldn't fathom it myself, until I could.) My mom tells me all my grandma remembered of her father were his beautiful green eyes, which seem to live on in my uncle Ray and my mother and were passed on to my brother, Brian, with whom they died.

My grandma didn't follow the example of her own mother and moved with my grandpa, Raymond, from Brooklyn out to Long Island, to the north shore hamlet of Smithtown, where they lived among Italian neighbors rumored to have mafia connections and certainly to have owned pizzerias. A true city girl, she couldn't drive and never learned, leaving her to be cooped up in the house with five kids. By the time I was around, she'd often lie on the couch and read cookbooks, absorb cookbooks, and cook. We'd spend days in bed, where on her nightstand was a plastic statue of the Virgin Mary filled with holy water, and watch Julia Child and *The Frugal Gourmet* on PBS, *The Elephant Show* on Nickelodeon. Grandpa worked as an engineer, often in the city, but he knew they could either live well in the suburbs or be stretched for survival in Brooklyn. And so they lived well, or at least that's how it always looked to me.

I remember her as someone wonderful, jolly: a cross between Cinderella's fairy godmother and Ina Garten. But there was her refusal to go to the doctor, which was why she died of cancer so young, at fifty-eight in 1991, leaving me the only grandchild to remember her and the fruit dusted in sugar. I'd been growing suspicious after visiting her in the hospital and, seemingly a few days later, seeing my aunts and uncles in black clothing. My uncle Rich, in a suit, looking so sad, coming up the same stairs my grandma had called down to my grandpa to go buy lamb chops—nothing was right. When they told me she'd passed, I didn't know how to react and pressed my face into my mother's straightened black hair. My dad was crying, and my grandpa, who delivered the news, looked so different. "Your hair is hot," I told my mom, wanting to distract from this new reality, overwhelmed as a five-year-old by the finality of death, if I even understood what it meant. I didn't think we were supposed to talk about it, about her; I swallowed my grief in fear of adult emotions. But I spent every Christmas of my childhood assuming my grandma would emerge, tell us that she'd just been hiding.

When my grandmother passed and I was no longer served a banquet on a daily basis while my parents were at work, food was neither fraught nor feared. Food was uncomplicated; everything else was charged. This was because there always was enough to eat in the house, ensured by my mom. Snacks, too, often Oreos, Chips Ahoy!, my brother's favorite Swiss Rolls of chocolate cake wrapped around thick whipped cream with that thinner than thin coating of hardened chocolate. The telltale white-and-blue box of Entenmann's—a Long Island staple once it made its move out from Brooklyn, the same trajectory as my maternal grandparents—always sat on the top of the fridge or microwave. I'd eat anything that came in this box, even basic powdered doughnuts and yellow cake with a thick chocolate fudge frosting you could peel off whole (a boring favorite of my brother's boring palate is how I saw it), but my favorite would come to be the Devil's Food Crumb, a chocolate cake doughnut coated in a layer of sweet crackly glaze and little beads of more cake on top. "Mommy!" I still gasp when I see them at Meat Farms, ready to beg, as though I couldn't just buy them myself. Proust had his madeleine; everyone who grew up in New York has their Entenmann's.

Fast food was a regular occurrence, regarded as a convenience as well as an indulgence, a pleasure. Chicken nuggets in barbecue sauce were my order, never a burger; I had a distaste for plastic-looking American cheese and squishy bread that remains part of the short list of things I won't eat (the exceptions of French brioche and Japanese milk bread would come much later). I never felt the weight of lack. My uncle Ray and I would race to see who could eat a Friendly's Reese's Peanut Butter Cup sundae faster (I think he might have let me win). We had gallons of whole milk with the red cap in the fridge at all times, picked up down the block at Dairy Barn with my mom's Marlboro Lights; she never fell under the spell of a fad diet, and so I only encountered that strain of nineties thought at sleepovers, when watery nonfat milk was poured over my morning cereal much to my discontent: Milk was supposed to be opaque, a pristine white—the very definition of that absence of color. I learned not to trust the lavender or blue caps on the white jugs. A family with this color was distinct from my own; I understood that immediately. These were folks who had taken seriously the fear of fat permeating U.S. culture, something I learned about while watching *Oprah* after school, eating a sleeve of Oreos. The red cap gave me a sense of superiority through its differentiation—*in my house, we eat well*; *in my house, the milk is the color it's supposed to be.* This was my mom's call, and it was my grandma's influence—she was always present in my mom's food, in her curiosity about ingredients and preparations, in the fact that she cared that we be nourished with both nutrition and pleasure.

My mom's family, with her four siblings, was a suburban ideal in her retellings, with summers spent at the maternal family home in Bay Ridge. Her uncle Freddy made plum jam—Betty's Jam, named for my grandma—at a factory in Red Hook; he liked my mom even if he only took her brothers with him to Coney Island, for which she still seems to be wounded. "No girls allowed because he couldn't take me to the bathroom," she recalls, but the good memories far outweigh the bad: getting the paper on 86th Street on Saturday evenings and going into the city to visit for holidays. Everyone in that house spoke German, yet as New Yorkers, it was Yiddish that flowed more seamlessly into my mom's and thus my vernacular. The concept of a "nosh" is as ingrained in me as my own name.

—

As I grew up and farther away from the time I spent with my grandma, food continued to be the most significant part of my days—the thing that could make or break my mood—and I had a relationship to it that was loose and unbothered. I was never told by family to stop eating, to worry over my body and how food might affect it, but I had observed early that this was something important to other people, something other people worried about maybe more than anything else. I was put into dance classes starting when I was at the tail end of three years old, which served as my crash course in gender. This was where I met my first friend, and we'd get taken to lunch with our moms. "You two are going to have to marry rich men," my friend's mother would say. "Men who can afford to feed you." I'd eye my mother, searching for approval or disapproval in her face. She'd give a gentle eye roll and tight smile, which I interpreted as my immunity from this sentiment. I made sure to eat every crumb on my plate. It might have been because we were growing children in strangely serious dance rehearsals that made us so hungry—that wasn't important here, though, and I already resented the implication of future dependence.

It was in the brightly lit, wooden-floored rooms of the dance school where I found out being a girl meant performing some specific behaviors. It was my introduction to the notion of "daintiness," a word I've never been able to inhabit. Ballet was a strange and confusing landscape: a place, a practice, a dance form where we needed to be strong and focused while keeping ourselves soft. Inner thighs burn in repeated pliés with feet set in first position while the arm goes up and over, requiring the strength of the shoulders and biceps. The core stays tight in its position, belly button to the spine, allowing straight posture. All the while, the neck gives a light tilt and the wrist has a studied limpness, and the fingers, they roll from joint to tip and back again like the gentle wave of a small bay. Point the toe; move into second position. Make it look effortless, make it look beautiful, while every muscle in the body is at work. Yes, this was training not for dance but for femininity. That was why we weren't supposed to enjoy our fries with such abandon. Abandon would be embarrassing; too much pleasure, obscene. Control, control, control while spinning; soutenu across the room, eyes set on something somewhere in the distance to avoid dizziness. To spin without getting dizzy, to hurt without a grimace, to exert without hunger. Girlhood.

My friend who also loved to eat would eventually be put in plastic pants for class, in the hope that they would make her sweat more and lose weight. A leotard and pink tights were the right of girls who could keep themselves in check.

This was part of a long legacy in the United States of worrying over fat as unbecoming, unattractive, and indeed a moral failing—especially on women. I watched my friend in dance class be put in those plastic pants out of the hope that she would shrink down. When I got to high school, where the nuns of my parochial grade school were replaced by Franciscan monks, there were girls in the bathrooms talking about their weight—about diets, about scales. I had thought we'd been saved from these concerns by feminism: In the late nineties, I was obsessed with Janeane Garofalo, *Daria*, and Margaret Cho. I thought women and girls could be smart, acerbic, and without makeup or concern for what boys liked. How wrong I was, how naïve it sounds now. But they were my models.

The physicality of dance never bothered me; it was the demands of performance, of the requirement that we smile not just onstage, but in after-school class. The expectation of a beautiful performance has always been my trouble with femininity. If I was going to smile, I'd need a reason. If I owed the world my happiness, I needed something in return. I wasn't supposed to think like this, and ballet class was supposed to train me out of the expectation. None of the girls in class with me would go on to be professional dancers, prima ballerinas at Juilliard or performing in *The Nutcracker* at Lincoln Center. Ballet class was a wholesome activity and a gender boot camp.

—

Despite delicious food always being important to my mother and something she always ensured we were eating, she didn't want me to learn how to cook. I hadn't expressed much interest in the kitchen beyond stuffing my face with whatever came out of it and standing in front of the refrigerator eating cold leftover sesame chicken and pork dumplings from the Chinese restaurant down the block. I would bake, because baking was fun and frivolous, or on occasion make something elaborate like a leg of lamb for my mom's birthday one year, yet the daily doings of meal-making and nutritional composition seemed like drudgery. It was a drudgery I'd seen my mom take on: "You'll spend your life doing it," she told me. "For a man." The venom of that last part, from someone who never made any feminist avowals, struck me like lightning: If having to make dinner every day could turn my mom into someone who names the patriarchy when usually she seemed rather politically disinterested, then there must be no fate worse.

The heteronormativity of this assumption aside, I took her advice to heart, because aside from my grandma, I'd never seen women truly happy in the kitchen unless they were on television. Men took on cooking for intellectual or creative reasons, and they enjoyed professional success through restaurant kitchens—even the ones on TV, like Bobby Flay and Emeril, had that chef-whites' sheen of lived-in expertise; meanwhile, women like Ina Garten, Giada De Laurentiis, and Rachael Ray were tasked with making women's misery somehow more palatable and easy, as far as I could tell. They put a happy face on the unpaid labor of domesticity. As a young adolescent, I knew who I'd rather be, the kind of future I'd rather pursue: the professional one, always depicted in opposition to the domestic, except for when I wanted to impress with a flan or towering sponge cake, with which I'd shock a coterie of eccentric and fabulous friends. Once I was old enough to have dreams about my future beyond "astronaut," it was "magazine editor" that was in my sights. This fantasy of a magazine editor would have her dinner parties catered.

"Whenever a domestic scientist wanted to emphasize the feminine side of the profession," writes Laura Shapiro in *Perfection Salad: Women and Cooking at the Turn of the Century*, "the adjective 'dainty' appeared." This word was meant to uplift the role of cooking, something previously reserved for servants, in social life. If one could get dirty in the kitchen while retaining her womanly wiles, her softness, then the kitchen was no longer a space of labor. And making kitchen and other domestic labor invisible was a core part of allowing women to participate, differentiating that work-work was something men did outside the home for money while women in the home were simply performing their duties. "We aim at giving others pleasure by obliterating the traces of our labor," writes Rosalind Coward in *Female Desires:*

How They Are Sought, Bought and Packaged. "Cooking food and presenting it beautifully is an act of servitude," she also says in the chapter on "food pornography," comparing how men seek visual titillation in sexual porn to women reading recipes. The only desires women can freely express, she says, is this desire to serve. They cannot indulge their desires themselves, whether for food or sex. It's always about being looked at, as object or server.

Lightness, daintiness, servitude, performance—these were the traditional feminine values I was noting as a young girl in ballet, and they were nothing that I could relate to and nothing I wanted to inhabit. They seemed utterly in contrast to the joyful indulgence in food that I was endlessly drawn to. To cook, I understood, would mean more performance of joy and care for the sake of others. Despite how much I loved to eat, I didn't see how cooking could be an expression of my real creativity or desires. It was because I could only see freedom in the posture of masculinity, and, as far as I could tell, men didn't do the family cooking. My father certainly didn't. They weren't asked to serve or smile when they didn't feel like it.

My official gender lashing-out began with asking my mom to buy me every shirt that said "girl power" when the Spice Girls were at their peak; it continued in middle school, predictably, with my fascination for the industrial rock of Nine Inch Nails and the wearing of electric-blue lip gloss when I wasn't in my Catholic school uniform. The blue lip gloss sounded the death knell of my ballet career. I liked boys, was obsessed with their apparent blankness: These were the people I was supposed to impress? They expressed so little, seemed to desire so little out of life. I didn't realize at the time that this was patriarchy and masculine norms working on them. Excitement and enthusiasm weren't for them, though they could be rambunctious. Once puberty hit, these roles seemed to solidify: Where in elementary school, we all played together at recess, whether breaking out into teams for kickball or on the swings, once we arrived to the middle grades, the boys played games and the girls stood in cliquish circles to gossip. (I was often standing in punishment at what was called "the wall," for having forgotten to do some part of my homework, distracted as I was by music videos.)

These lessons that I didn't consider lessons at the time, simply a flurry of observations and reactions, were imparting upon me that I didn't want to be one of the mothers at my brother's baseball games, handing out orange slices and Hi-C on the sidelines. ("You're just like recording all the time when you're a kid—you don't miss anything," the poet Eileen Myles told an interviewer once. "And writing is when you kind of grow up and you put a voice-over onto all those recordings.") I still wonder when I was supposed to accept marriage and motherhood as my sacred duty. I bristled at our lessons in religion classes about staying "neat," not succumbing to fashion trends, and remaining a virgin until marriage. All of this seemed, simply put, uncool—in contrast to the messages I got watching my beloved music videos on the supposedly "indie" version of MTV called M2.

Mass did nothing for me; Deftones did everything. (Shove it, shove it, shove it—amen.) I knew what I wanted to be, and it was in opposition to all of the values being force-fed down my throat; I knew this was possible because I'd seen Manhattan—I'd seen the city, which I imagined as full of magazine editors going to art shows and dining at cafés—and I was reading novels where the main characters also felt as bad as I did in the suburbs.

On one family excursion to the city, I saw a woman dressed all in black with a knot of lavender hair on top of her head chatting with someone on the street. "That will be Alicia," my mom said as we drove past, again gently granting me permission to be myself, and I've never forgotten her. She became the symbol of a future free of nuns, ballet, and jokes about marrying a man rich enough to buy me a steak dinner; she became the symbol of a future where people didn't think I was bad just because I was a girl who didn't want to smile for no reason, a girl who wanted to read different books than were assigned. There were blueprints for the kind of life I wanted—I just didn't know anyone who had built from them. But there were people who did, and the woman with the lavender hair was my evidence. That woman, I was sure, didn't cook.

And so to be that woman, to be the fabulous magazine editor of my dreams, I thought I'd have to do the same: to reject the angel in the house. My mom knew—that's why she told me not to learn how to cook: reject the angel's siren call of a simple domestic life, the angel's complaints about my unwieldiness and refusal to please men, the angel's slapping of my hand away from another serving at dinner. Virginia Woolf spoke about her, this dainty woman who is soft, kind, doesn't make a fuss about herself. "If there was chicken, she took the leg," wrote Woolf, in her 1931 speech "Professions for Women," meaning this ideal homemaker would take the least meaty part for herself and leave the rest for everyone else. I could never accept that; I was too hungry, all the time, for both food and experience.

Woolf hoped that younger women wouldn't know her, this ghost of a Victorian past, yet she lives on—has perhaps only gotten stronger by being allowed to hide in feminisms of "choice." Barbie was a feminist, or so I've read, because there was no kitchen in the dream house. She was a product of a mid-century dream that a woman would be more than a housewife, more than the sum of her domestic labor. "By the mid-1940s, the American food industry had a single overriding ambition: to create a mass market for the processed food that had been developed originally to feed the armed forces," writes Shapiro in an essay called "Do Women Like to Cook?" As more women were pushed into the labor force, a new market was created—more money was to be made by corporations, and they were calling it feminism, because who really wanted to cook? Not Barbie.

—

The question of whether to choose domesticity or art is so commonplace as to be dull, yet it persists because of the necessity of each. This necessity has led to the desperate notion of the "art monster" in Jenny Offill's 2014 novel *Dept. of Speculation*: The central rejection of the art monster would be the duties of domesticity as wife and mother, of which cooking is part. Lauren Elkin writes in *Art Monsters: Unruly Bodies in Feminist Art* that "the monstrous gives us these new words and methods which help us move past a conception of women's storytelling that binds us doubly into shame or empowerment, loyalty or betrayal, silence or freedom, domesticity or art. We don't live in these binaries; not really."

We don't live in them, and despite all the joy I took in food, I had lumped cooking in with all the other unfair expectations of my gender. I wanted to be smart and funny, rigorous and ruthless. Cooking couldn't be part of that, surely. It was something you did either because you loved it or you had to, and women always seemed to have to. My earliest model of the cook was my grandma, who cooked because she loved it and because she had to; she had to and did it with curiosity and love anyway. So did my mom, a lot of the time, who came home from a full-time job each day to prepare meals. These meals, her meals, were the light of an upbringing in which I otherwise felt alienated, adrift, and under the thumb of my father's demands for a seemingly unachievable perfection.

—

When I first began cooking in my early twenties, I wanted to do so in the mode of a male chef: a hobby, all technique and no love. I'm grateful for that education, for my obsession with scales over volume measures and my knowledge of how to make a proper paté de fruit (even if I haven't bought a Brix meter to measure the sugar percentage precisely). Inevitably, though, cooking becomes care: for self, for others. Often, this care-cooking, this simplicity is rooted in nourishment and satisfaction and nostalgia for the flavors that represented love for us when we were children; it's not about properly measuring the sugar on the Brix meter but getting the balance of tart cream cheese to rich butter to powdered sweetness just right in grandma's carrot cake frosting.

I collect sentences by women writers where they talk of how the domestic has ensnared their would-be compatriots in work, art, travel, fucking. Who is doing the tasks, then, of life? Who is buying the groceries, cooking the meals, and scrubbing the tiles if not the women themselves? The implication is that these are outsourced tasks, paid for and considered beneath the working woman who has freed herself from the shackles of the stove. Domesticity—a trap of dull necessities unless you can pay your way out of it, unless someone else is scrubbing and sweating and chopping the mirepoix, searing the steak, frying the frites. Or maybe I'm getting ahead of myself, imagining this bistro meal. Maybe someone else is merely making the boxed macaroni and cheese, which is cooking, too—just be sure to give it a nice sprinkling of fresh cracked pepper to serve.

New dichotomies emerge for the woman who cooks, even when she's made it a trade, a profession, a craft, and is paid for her expertise, making it work-work. Cooking in a chef's mode rather than a care mode also seemed a rejection of what was supposed to be my place: I wanted power and to believe I had power, so I had to pretend that my gender didn't determine who I was and could be, and certainly that it didn't determine how and what I ate. What that meant in reality was that I was simply mimicking men and masculinity; what it meant was that I'd internalized misogyny down to my very taste buds, the thing I'd always prided myself on. I'd been all about girl power; I'd really tried to make myself something in opposition to what the dominant culture was telling me to be: pretty, not smart; obsessed with thinness; dainty, not strong. I was proud of how big a steak I could eat just like I was proud that my softball coaches implored me not to throw the ball from shortstop to first base with such force. I didn't eat or throw like a girl—I still couldn't see that these didn't make me as free as I thought they would.

I was taught to eat like a girl-king by women, through care and love, and I was rejecting the significance of their work. I was warned not to learn how to cook by my own mother, and I began cooking anyway. Learning how to cook was, for me, like taking a bite of a forbidden apple: I was told not to, that it would doom me. Instead, the world broke open.

On Apples

OVER TIME, THROUGH EATING ONE APPLE AFTER another, I came to be. My taste for them accumulated, like the books, songs, and movies I collected in order to make myself a person who would be worthy of the city and of magazine jobs. I took notes, and I was sure of my taste.

—

Malus domestica—the Latin name for the more than 7,500 known cultivars of what we know in English as an apple. It translates directly to *bad domestic*, which brings to mind some scrapped Pedro Almodóvar script about a long-suffering housewife daring to spike a tarta de manzana to serve a cheating husband. Does the name come from our precedent or does the name simply suit our stories a bit too neatly? Apples figure into so much mythology, across cultures and spiritualities: a golden apple dropped by the Greek goddess Eris, leading to the Trojan War; Eve in the garden, tempted as she was by Satan; in the fairy tale where a naïve and hungry Snow White is served a poisoned apple by her evil stepmother in disguise. For a long time, in many languages, the word for "apple" served as a stand-in for all fruit. It is indeed a human point of genesis, so common to be almost trite as subject matter. Its foundational role as fruit and story, though, makes it too tempting.

There's treachery in these grand narratives of the apple that speaks to a ubiquity that transforms into trustworthiness. So normal is it to find an apple and to rely on it as a quick snack, even in the rare climates where palatable ones don't easily grow, that one would never consider that it could be a portal to war, sin, or endless sleep. In a purée, they're often the first fruit many babies are introduced to, good for their vitamin C, helping the newborns absorb iron. Apples can be the first taste after mother's milk. They play a fascinating dual role, then, in our imaginations: something utterly safe; something to be wary of. "It was an apple of discord only because it was an apple of love," wrote Eugene Stock McCartney in 1925, of the dropped fruit that began the Trojan War. We've been trying to figure out what this fruit really means for so long: What it represents might just be this endless complication, the impossibility of disentangling love and trust from the vulnerable possibility of betrayal. As we contemplate, we eat, and hope we aren't greeted by a worm.

Apples are of the family *rosaceae*, which also includes roses, quince, pears, strawberries, cherries, almonds, raspberries, and more of the most commonly cultivated plants we know as food and ornament. The apple specifically originated in Kazakhstan, located in Central Asia, and by 1500 BCE, they'd spread throughout Europe. Though there are over 7,500 varieties that we know about, just twenty types of apple account for 90 percent of all eaten. These were chosen not for being crowned the most delicious, but for being hardy to the elements, grown at volume, and able to travel long distances without unsightly bruising. Since the dawn of the industrialization of agriculture, these have been bigger deciding factors in what food makes it to us than whether it's interesting or tasty.

The trees are heterozygotes: Each new plant is, really, a new species. They reproduce like people, in that way, where a cross-pollination from two parents produces something similar but altogether new. This is useful evolutionarily speaking—it accounts for the spread of the fruit and people far and wide, in so many soils—but it hadn't been good for commercial production. That's where the cultivars have come in, with grafting of branches onto rootstock in order to replicate the desired apple over and over.

—

My parents—my cross-pollinators—married in October of 1984: my mom was twenty-one, my dad twenty-two. I came along thirteen months later. Though he'd harbored dreams of being a lawyer, my dad dropped out of college, no longer able to afford the tuition, and like a lot of thwarted lawyers, became a cop—a New York state trooper, donning purple ties and gray cowboy hats. He'd grown up in the Stephen Wise Towers at 117 West 90th Street, public housing, the child of Rosa and Edward Kennedy. Rosa had come to New York City from Puerto Rico in the 1940s and never looked back; the long, bumpy ride on a small plane curing her of ever entertaining the idea of boarding one again. Edward was born upstate and raised in the Bronx, child of an Irish father and German mother; I'm told we could've been like the rich kind of Kennedys had my great-grandfather gone to church, but he had a taste for alcohol and cigarettes, and he married a German woman named Magdalena Müller, so my grandfather and his siblings were kept away from their cousins, having sullied the good family line. Both of my paternal grandparents were bilingual, my grandmother a native Spanish speaker and my grandfather having learned German from his mother; neither passed these languages on, though they would emerge under the influence of drink or stress.

Rosa was reserved, not the type of loving grandmother one imagines—the kind I was lucky to have even so briefly through my mom's mom. I didn't call her abuela; she didn't make me tostones. I remember my grandfather, a long-distance runner who nonetheless died of a heart attack in 1996, as a man who loved to tan, who died with a full head of white hair, and who wore rubber bands around his wrist for reasons I could never discern, though it was a habit my brother picked up.

Like my maternal grandparents, they'd lived in the city most of their lives, and they didn't move out to the suburbs until my dad was eighteen, raising my aunt Susan, uncle Steven, and father Brian in the projects. Rosa worked as a nurse's aide at Columbia-Presbyterian Hospital, often taking on late shifts that my dad says always kept him up nights, waiting for her safe return. Edward coached the kids' baseball teams and played in Central Park softball leagues; there's a photo of him posing in position to field. My dad, as a kid, flew pigeons from the rooftop, but nothing was idyllic about the living situation: Over years, stories trickled out here and there of jumping roofs and watching a friend fall to his death; having a cop pull a gun on him as a child in the elevator; priests who groomed altar boys for sexual abuse; and his siblings' ongoing issues with drugs. My father, the cop, had two older siblings for whom I often answered the phone and heard, "This is a collect call from a correctional facility..."

Their house was the opposite of the splendor of my maternal grandma's; there wasn't much exciting food to speak of, but there was a constant supply of Sugar Smacks cereal. The biggest difference is that there, I wasn't considered the least bit special. The only time I enjoyed being in their home was when my grandmother started to talk about growing up in Puerto Rico—a place where both her parents died before she was ten years old and where her brother Domingo was murdered at sixteen, so she didn't like to talk about it much. When she was orphaned, she'd gone to live with her aunt, who made her money as a psychic, practicing Santería, an African diasporic tradition that blends Yoruba with Catholicism. "The house would shake as she spoke to the dead,"

Rosa would tell me, outside at the metal table on the concrete patio in their backyard. "Tell me more!" I'd beg, but she wouldn't. I'd recount this to my father later, and he'd be surprised she'd mentioned it at all. The only evidence of her origins in the house was one small Puerto Rican flag—the blue of it the dark navy of U.S. empire, not the light blue of hoped-for liberation. I wanted to know more of this place, which seemed to me both exotic and wildly fun.

Edward and Rosa moved out to Long Island when my father was finishing high school, and he'd go on to enroll at the local college SUNY Farmingdale, where my parents would meet in a statistics class. They married young, and I'd say stupidly if that wouldn't imply my own existence is stupid. My brother, Brian, came in 1990, my sister, Cameron, in 2000—a surprise, a gift, and the reason I've long known I don't need to have a child; I know what that's like. We always lived in Patchogue, a south shore town that had been a working-class fishing and manufacturing village, and now is bustling and expensive. The once-small Blue Point Brewery's expansion since the late nineties into an Anheuser-Busch behemoth has marked its evolution into a haven of mostly bad restaurants and pricey apartments. Our first home was a small white two-bedroom house with a huge backyard that provided the setting for all of my playing pretend. I climbed its trees to sit in and hide, and from there I'd spy on neighbors' yards. Eventually, we moved to a bigger house in 1994, where I finally got my own room: the only room upstairs, carved out of the attic, meaning total privacy because I could always hear if someone was coming up the stairs (and they rarely did) and rush to adjust my behavior (meaning, hide my diary). It would be the sanctuary of my adolescence, where I journaled and listened to Duncan Sheik on my boom box; these would be the walls I covered in printed out photos of Savage Garden, every single photo on the internet that was then not so infinite. It would be where I made a shrine to John Frusciante and eventually become addicted to caffeine during a college Red Bull phase.

—

Henry David Thoreau published the piece "Wild Apples" in *The Atlantic* at the end of his life. All the way back in 1862, he was already lamenting the loss of savage apples to be found while walking and eaten in the fresh wind for the sake of cultivated orchards made by human design. Apples had been spread throughout the world by both human and animal, the seeds themselves being unique for spreading untouched through animal feces. Cows and birds, thus, would often be growing their own food, feasting on ripe and fallen fruit while also keeping the trees clipped. "Apples for grafting appear to have been selected commonly, not so much for their spirited flavor, as for their mildness, their size, and bearing qualities—not so much for their beauty, as for their fairness and soundness," Thoreau wrote. "Indeed, I have no faith in the selected lists of pomological gentlemen."

Pomological gentlemen! These are the cultivated apples, the ones we've come to know over centuries as they moved from Central Asia to Greece, Rome, England, and then the rest of the world. They're "tame and forgettable," according to Thoreau; they're without "*tang* or *smack*." Yet these are what we know, unless we go seeking wild fruit for ourselves.

—

The phrase "as American as apple pie" takes on new meaning when we consider that, like new Americans born of European stock and settling upon indigenous lands, all apples but crabapples came to this land as immigrants and were naturalized. M.F.K. Fisher in a 1975 *Esquire* piece titled "Apple Pie" asserts as much, noting the phrase is as meaningless as saying "proudly that a Swedish or Irish grandfather who emigrated to Minnesota was 'a first American.' Both the pie and the parent sprang from other cultures, and neither got here before the Indian." They assimilated so well that they're a national symbol.

A quintessential American tale was built around Johnny Appleseed, whom I half-believed was a fictional character. I'd only seen him rendered as a cartoon in children's books, but he was real: named John Chapman, he planted acres of apple orchards across the country that were used for making hard cider. It wasn't until Prohibition that apples became more commonly grown for eating than for making into alcohol. What Chapman did in the early nineteenth century was travel west before settlers and plant orchards he'd then sell to newcomers. He was a member of the Swedenborgian Church, which didn't allow grafting, thus requiring him to plant his orchards from seed. These were the wild style apples favored by Thoreau, which weren't really desirable for eating unless you were wandering by foot for long periods. They would become cider.

Though the United States has done a good and unsurprising job of usurping the story of this fruit—one that is generally agreeable and appealing, one that spreads through a sort of pioneer mentality—apples are a global commodity. China produces more apples than the U.S. They grow in "places as different as Turkey and Norway," according to *Apple: A Global History*. For this reason, apples seem to me a point of connection rather than difference. Whenever greeted with phrases like this—"places as different as . . . "—especially around something like an apple, which has been proven to grow in most of the world, I think, *Why aren't we focused on the similarities?* If there's common ground in common fruit, why the consistent focus on difference and lines drawn by human-made borders? My fractured ethnic heritage might give me this love for the liminal and in between, the ambiguous and poorly defined, but it's also my mom's influence: She learned how to cook plantains from my Puerto Rican aunt Sally, rice balls from a friend's Italian mother, matzoh balls from a co-worker's Jewish wife. Food was always multicultural and interpersonal, with deliciousness the common denominator. Apples don't make me see divides; they make me see a common taste, a common value.

They are central to stories in Celtic, Norse, and Greek mythology, and would become significant in Christianity and Islam as well as in fairy tales. Snow White eats the poisoned apple, of course; King Arthur is revived by golden apples on the magical island of Avalon. Idun, keeper of apples, is a goddess of Norse myth; the gods must eat of her apples to retain their youth and immortality. The role of the apple would be diverse across these narratives: here, representing fertility; there, longevity. It would become a symbol of the emerging twin religions of the twentieth century: capital and technology. New York was named "the Big Apple" for being the place where one can make their fortune, and Steve Jobs named his minimal-aesthetic computer company after the fruit.

Fertility, female sexuality, and desire have been central to the ways in which the apple has been used symbolically in various cultures: It's almost always about women, about our desire and whether we're in competition to be the most youthful, the most beautiful. Idun, keeper of apples; Eve, eater of the cursed one. What are we promised through an apple? Who can we be by biting into one? Which portals will we open, and will they bring about a dramatic demise?

—

Though so few apple cultivars have been popular in the U.S., that has changed. While Red Delicious, Gala, Granny Smith, Fuji, and the like have long been standards, the emergence of Honeycrisp from a breeding program at the University of Minnesota in the early 1990s showed that there were still new flavors to be found in this staple fruit. Desirable apples, with their unique textures, flavors, and juiciness, are trademarked and come to join our personal palate libraries.

Apples taught me how to taste. My association with them is not so deep, not so rife with metaphor at first glance: The ease of finding different varieties allowed me a smooth introduction to small differences in flavor, texture, size, and color; all of these influenced my experience of the fruits, teaching me discernment in a small-stakes way. I never liked a mealy Red Delicious, nor a tart Granny Smith. The just-right McIntosh—sweet and firm, with a barely-there touch of acidity, and that pretty, seemingly airbrushed skin so gently shifting in color from red to green: This was my apple.

Was the first opinion I was allowed to have the refusal of an apple that wasn't to my liking? Perhaps, then, my apples weren't too out of step with their symbolic use. With apples, I could name my desire. I would go forth into the world confident of one thing, and it's that I prefer a McIntosh. *And here are my reasons...* I've always loved to tell people precisely why I like or dislike different types of fruits, and I've learned over time that there will be many people who don't want to hear anything of it. My palate doesn't interest them; seemingly small distinctions don't interest them; food doesn't interest them. These are the people to whom I have nothing to say.

In eighth grade, I was requesting admissions materials from colleges in the city as soon as I could access the internet and reading *Trainspotting*, with all its filth and written in a Scottish dialect I could barely understand. My copy of the Irvine Welsh novel had images from its movie adaptation on its cover, with Ewan McGregor soaking wet. (Ewan McGregor soaking wet, not my passion for inventive literature, might have been why I wanted this book.) Sister Dorothy picked it up one day while I was in the bathroom, and upon my return, she beckoned me with her wrinkled fingers and whispered into my ear, her breath always stinking of the coffee that stained her teeth brown, "The language in here is very bad. The word 'cunt'—it's very offensive to women. Do your parents know you're reading this?" she asked. "My mom bought it for me," I told her, which was the truth, and she wrote home a note that I pretended was for the far less offensive *Less Than Zero*. Sister Dorothy, my middle school nemesis, also told my new best friend, Kerry, that it was good we'd be going to different high schools, because I was a bad influence: The book with the foul language was the most clear evidence of this.

That my mother bought me the books with the offensive language and a Tinky Winky backpack, the stuffed character on a children's show who was facing right-wing backlash for supposedly being gay, suggested a tacit support for my minor disobediences. It was always she who went up to the school to complain of mistreatment while my father would have taken the side of authority. He was the reason I was in this Catholic school to begin with, even though he never took Communion on the rare occasions he came with us to Mass. "I haven't confessed," he'd name as the reason. My aunt Susan, his sister, had begun to be what he'd interpreted as wayward in these years of her life; for whatever reason, it seems that he assumed I, in the suburbs, was similarly at risk of a life of drugs and criminality.

What Catholic school did was give urgency to all my tiny rebellions, which took place mainly within my mind and in my journals purchased at Hot Topic or through the Delia*s catalog. I had always been a good girl in the grand scheme of things, not even at risk of smoking a cigarette because they were bad for you, yet I was constantly receiving pushback—the insistence that I harbored a latent darkness that needed to be kept in check.

Now, in retrospect, it's said that I just always was good—always did the right thing. The truth is that I was terrified not to: I cried in first grade the first time I got a 90 instead of 100 on a spelling test, thinking my dad would kill me. Resentment brewed inside me from a young age of how perfect I thought I had to be, and of how much evidence I saw in my own family of the ways in which straying from that perfection could destroy my life. There was no gray area that I could see. Intellectually, I refused to believe that I was bad because I knew I wasn't; emotionally, it was taking a toll to have the way I was treated be so disconnected to what I knew was reality. Between Sister Dorothy at school and a domineering father at home, I felt like I could never get anything right, but I also didn't want to do things "right" by the standards I thought of as bullshit. Apples and friendships, books and college admissions catalogs, Tinky Winky and Hot Topic—these were how I began to cultivate my own desires.

Tasting different varieties was and is an ongoing learning

experience—the formative one, the one that made me feel the flow of information from tongue to brain. Once I knew what that felt like, there were no limits to the potential I could unlock just by eating. I'd been driven by simple hungers prior to my discernment between apples. I wanted to gnaw on the fat off a steak. I wanted to crack into a lobster's shell and suck out its meat. I wanted the bites of stuffed green olive in my mother's pastelillos and to burn my tongue on plantain chips fresh from oil. I knew what I wanted when it came to food, but I never put too much thought to why: These pleasures were obvious, primal, based in desires for fat, salt, and carbohydrates.

Apples were so much more than that. They taught me that food comes from the ground, not a supermarket. During Long Island falls, before it was the right time to go pumpkin picking for Halloween decorations, we would pick apples off trees at an orchard. These were different all the time, depending on when my mom wanted to follow one of the many hand-painted signs advertising rows of trees. We'd exit the highway and be on our way to fill up a bushel. Ramshackle wooden farmstands would have apple cider doughnuts and pies and piles of squash for sale. We had to drive about forty-five minutes from my dead and dormant hometown to find it, but here was an autumn harvest.

Upon returning home, I remember my mother giving a sigh when she plopped the overflowing paper sack of our apples on the counter. In the apples, she didn't see any reason for excitement. They were another chore to take on, while she worked all day, made dinner, and did all the upkeep in the house. These apples were, to her, a glut and a burden; they were a pie to bake, something else to deal with, and I couldn't understand. To have so many apples seemed, to me, an opportunity: True to form, I'd snack on as many as I could.

At the supermarket, though, I would beg for pineapples and coconuts. (Eventually, in the tropical Caribbean, I'd long for the apples.) I only truly appreciated them when we got them ourselves, piled into bushels, some of them with their leaves still attached to the stem. Those were and are still my favorite, the ones that show signs of where they come from. I want to admire them, photograph them.

—

My parents' marriage very rapidly ended after twenty-five years in 2009. The telltale sign was that my mom stopped making mashed potatoes from scratch, opting for the instant kind; the labor she'd always put in to keeping a well-fed and perfunctorily happy home was no longer viable: It wouldn't last until my sister's eighteenth birthday, a decade away. Every day, her sighs were weighed down now, like when we'd come home from out east with too many apples.

She left the house I grew up in one early morning, with my sister in tow, after a final fight with my father, and I woke up one day to just my brother at home. He'd spent one semester at a punishing military school in South Carolina called the Citadel—my father's choice, more discipline as presumed antidote to the desperation to be seen, safe, and understood. I realized I was finally free in one way: If they were gone, I could go. Despite my longing for independence, I had always been the good girl waiting for permission. I had understood the lure of being the angel in the house, after all: It was a means of survival.

But in survival, I was languishing: a fruit unsuited to the environment. The temperate—the standard climate, according to the American imagination, which we know can run wild. It's standard, maybe, because it's where apples thrive most. They had been so plentiful and diverse by the time of the American Revolution, one in every ten farms in New England had a cider mill. It had been considered safer to drink than water and was even prescribed for ailments; this was a tradition brought over from England, where cider had such a central cultural role that after Christmas, in a holdover pagan practice, people would go "wassailing" to ensure a good harvest. In the U.S., the cider tradition died with Prohibition, and then came the focus on eating apples.

—

Now, on Long Island, some of that old appreciation for wild apples and their cider potential is being re-envisioned. Floral Terranes, a two-person wine- and cider-making team, has gone in search of what they call "suburban terroir." It's the bounty, the abundance I hadn't known was always underfoot on Long Island—underfoot and hanging over highways, in the case of some wild apples that have been turned into their dry ciders. The special maritime climate of the region provides minerality and saltiness. History and the future forged through foraging, reminding me that apples are indeed everywhere that people are—not just accessible through a special trip to be made at the right season, but wherever seeds are plopped.

This is important to me because I always thought of life as something that would happen elsewhere. Typical adolescent thinking, but gradually, I saw that there was life on Long Island, even if one had to really know where to look in order to find it. All that time I thought I could be somewhere else: My life was in the city, surely; the answers about my heritage, what I could really claim, were somewhere in Ireland and down in Puerto Rico. Patchogue was purgatory, I was convinced, and eventually I'd have the freedom and the money to find out who I really was. Once I left, I could see things clearly: I was home where I was born, where apples grow in rows and wild.

There had been so much I'd missed while focused on escape, even the scent of the fruit that taught me everything I know. When I read Thoreau wrote that some wild apples had such an intense fragrance that they would suffice as perfume if carried in one's handkerchief, I realized I'm nose-blind to apples. I don't know whether I've ever really smelled one, even when it comes to those fresh fall fruits picked from the trees myself. Was I just trained, as an American accustomed to the supermarket, to forget that fruit even has fragrance? Apples may have taught me to taste, but these have taught me there's more to the pleasure of fruit than just how it feels in the mouth.

—

This forgetting of scent when it came to apples, this erasure of it, reminds me that wild fruit has the potential to connect all the senses, to engage our desires. Throughout the centuries, fruit trees have been planted in public spaces to provide sustenance, shade, and invitations to community.

Public fruit seems simple, banal, but it contains possibility. Apples have long opened up our human worlds, connected us with the gods and goddesses. What portal might a new tree in the neighborhood open up? What future could those community connections build? Might we smell apples again, even if we've gotten so used to them that we forget they were ever supposed to have a scent, like all living things? If I were languishing in the suburbs, might I have just grown too accustomed to its scent, to its predictable texture?

Romans dined among fruit trees; Catholic monks grew fruit in their monasteries, so as not to have to leave to find food; for Protestants, orchards and botanical gardens were a means of repairing the damage of the Garden of Eden. As access to nature has been associated with better living and improved mental health, more widespread interest in public fruit and urban agriculture today speaks to a desire to reconnect through food to nature and community—to bring us back to that early moment in human civilization when planting fruit trees meant a home was being established, a home that could provide. Thoreau, in expressing an attachment to what we'd now call and commodify as "wellness," knew in 1862 that walking and picking fruit had the ability to brighten the soul as well as nourish the body.

When apples started to be cultivated at scale for their hardiness, in effect, that's when the city–rural divide became stronger. Urban agriculture, which has long been a significant food source in poorer countries and the global south, went out of fashion as food became produced more industrially and people went to work in factories. But in recent decades, it's been understood that city-based food systems can help communities become more resilient to the extreme weather of climate change and have the bonus of creating stronger human bonds. While only 15 to 20 percent of the global food supply is provided by urban agriculture, community gardens and public fruit projects enhance people's connection to place in addition to providing free fruits and vegetables for their diets.

—

The pleasure of a good apple can be a bridge toward the question of why not everything tastes so good, smells so fragrant. A good apple can teach us to trust our taste buds and learn, gradually, to trust ourselves.

There could be an eye-opening to apples as both easy to access and extremely special. Fresher fruit, so fragrant as to be a perfume of its own when carried, and free fruit, growing on highways and foraged to become a gorgeous cider or placed strategically in a city neighborhood for locals to enjoy, help me to remember that once upon a time, when I was a child, a bushel of apples in the kitchen may as well have been a pot of gold. Where once I would have thought to myself there's nothing more banal than apples, now I understand their potential—not just to travel the world, to grow wherever they find soil, but to connect me back to a self who found her words, her desire, through their freckled skin, firm flesh, and lively combination of sweet and tart. They were my portal to taste as a way of asserting myself, defining myself, as a gluttonous child with discerning tastes. To crave them now reminds me where I come from, no matter how far afield I try to go in search of myself.

On Chocolate

When Brian and I put on the well-worn VHS of *Willy Wonka and the Chocolate Factory*, I'd close my eyes during the introduction: Chocolate was being made, molded from hot liquid to bars, and it stirred within me too strong a craving for the taste. In Patchogue, there was no bodega at the street corner to run to for a Hershey's bar. Who knew when I'd get my next M&M? The way I gasp "Mommy!" when I see the Devil's Food Crumb Entenmann's doughnuts is this child emerging again through my throat, surprising me.

That kind of supermarket candy filled with sugar and barely containing any actual cacao was how I, like most American kids, established my obsession with the stuff. My grandpa Raymond came to all my dance recitals and orchestra concerts with a telltale gold box of Godiva truffles, and these were my true favorite—the sweets I coveted. The white chocolate starfish striped with milk chocolate and filled with raspberry jelly—oh, I can taste it right now.

Chocolate, the first true object of my longing and love, was the way I learned about exploitation in the global food system. I was always susceptible to a bit of greenwashing and virtue-signaling when it came to any commodities for sale. I didn't eat yogurt, but I knew that if I did, it'd be organic Stonyfield Farm, because their cows, I was assured, were very happy. Fruitopia, I was positive, had to be very good, better than Snapple, because its packaging suggested a funky, hippie vibe. Imagine my grown-up surprise when I learned it was always owned by Coca-Cola.

I fancied myself a progressive before I knew what that word was, but that didn't mean I understood economies of scale. When I started to see "fair trade" on different chocolate labels, I needed to know what that meant beyond the way I generally associated it with Bono and Coldplay—I'd put a "make trade fair" sticker that I picked up at a concert on my camera without knowing what the hell it actually meant—so I went to the primitive internet: It meant that the chocolate had been made with cacao harvested by folks who were adults and paid a living wage for their work, as opposed to the enslaved child labor on the Ivory Coast and other underpaid workers or exploited farmers that provided commodity chocolate for all the brands that had birthed my taste for cocoa. Doing my best to give up my beloved Snickers and Reese's Peanut Butter Cups and boxes of Godiva would be my first foray into trying to make my food choices match up with my politics. I didn't know that this was a dangerous train of thought that would derail the life I'd found myself living in survival mode.

—

When I was sixteen and enrolled one summer in a driver's ed class at the local public high school, I met a boy. While boys had been blank spaces for me to fill in with stories in my notebooks about the torment I felt at never having the guts to talk to them or fantasies about being swept off my feet, this one had become real: He and his extremely spiky hair, gelled into a solid state out of an allegiance to 2002 pop-punk fashion, would squeeze close to me in the back seat while our companions were in the driver's seat learning how to do three-point turns and merge onto the expressway. Todd was his name, and it was a name I liked, but I didn't know whether I liked him. This was the time of AOL Instant Messenger, and our romances and friendships played out through its text boxes, door-opening sounds, and away messages. Song lyrics told the stories of crushes or heartache. He'd switched into my car to be with his best friend and ended up next to me, asking a series of questions, to which I gave one-word answers, including "Do you have a boyfriend?" and "Do you like boys?" before asking for my screen name. I gave it to him, touched by his sensitivity to the possibility that I could be a lesbian.

I wrote about it in my LiveJournal, wondering whether I could give up the fake relationship I had with an oboe player who knew who Jeff Buckley was for this public school kid who loved emo bands with nasal-voiced singers that I thought sucked. He changed his screen name to "resting-sound" to reference a song by Midtown that conveyed his agony over the tumult I was putting him through: *I'm losing sleep, she's resting sound*. He persisted. Because of my appreciation of a public display of torment, and because he wanted to kiss me and I wanted to be kissed, Todd became my boyfriend. The strange thing is that he stayed my boyfriend for the next eleven years.

On our first date, he took me to see a community production of *The Music Man* at the Amphitheater at Bald Hill. For our second date, and the one I'd decide would be our anniversary, I took him with my best friends—still Kerry, despite Sister Dorothy, and Doug, a new friend I'd made in high school—on the Long Island Rail Road to go see *24 Hour Party People*, a Steve Coogan movie about the rise and fall of Factory Records, at Sunshine Cinemas on the Lower East Side. It was a demonstration of my worldliness for a person who didn't really need to be impressed. My friends didn't like him, and the same went for my parents: He was a bit odd, not all that cute, was one of those white guys who liked to play devil's advocate in conversation, and I'm not sure what we had in common aside from a shared interest in computers. For him, it was about how they worked; for me, it was about the world they connected me with beyond what I could find on Long Island. Regardless, I fell in love.

I liked being in the basement apartment where he lived

with his parents because they were hands-off in the way mine loomed over me, trying to make sure I didn't slip up despite no evidence that I was on any path but the straight and narrow. Since my sister had been born, my mom had her hands full with a new baby and my father had always been hands-off except as a disciplinarian or when we bonded over things like the greatness of "Love Will Tear Us Apart" by Joy Division: I had come to hide everything I was and wanted to be at home out of a fear of mockery or derision. My violin playing, my interest in photography—these weren't always nourished. Had I been an athlete like my brother, perhaps the story would have been different. In my attic room, I created a sanctuary with a boom box; at school, I relished being around my orchestra friends, the kind of people I'd always dreamed of meeting, who were silly, weird, and loved music as much as I did. Once I was no longer a child and had come into adolescence, I was rarely treated at home like a person but more like a time bomb counting down to some colossal fuck-ups. Regardless of how I behaved, which was as a garden variety daughter of both Catholic school and a cop—a rule follower who, in her head, spits on authority—I still never felt like I was good.

The girl who at sixteen went to driver's ed was always on edge about things like getting an 88 in math; Brian was under similar pressure, with the added stress of needing to be a star baseball player. Meanwhile, Todd's parents cracked open beers after work; they listened to Yes; they cooked canned green beans, and I liked the metallic tinge.

Todd hated the sound of their beer cans releasing air and vowed to always be straight-edge, abstaining from alcohol and drugs; considering my dad's siblings' problems, I saw nothing wrong with that. I wanted somewhere else to be, a world to disappear into. Here was a boy, real and present, and I was still using him as a blank space to mold into what I needed him to be, and what I needed him to be was an escape hatch. Despite my strong friendships, I'd internalized some idea that romance was the only secure way to insure against loneliness.

—

All my youthful dreams of freedom and new experiences still defined my hopes for the future, but I was hopelessly attached to this boy, this first love. I went to college in the city, as I'd always planned to do, at Fordham University in the Bronx. I'd spend my weekdays in class, at a nonsense work-study job, and going into Manhattan to buy CDs and browse magazines at Tower Records. When work-study checks came, I'd reward myself with an order of delivery Chinese food; when there were no work-study checks, I got the five-dollar combo at the student-famous Pugsley's Pizzeria: a chicken roll, a slice, and a soda. (It can't be five dollars anymore, can it?) I went to the cafeteria once before finding the food subpar and using all my dining hall allowance at a place that served crappy pizza and paninis. I made a performative ramen in the communal dorm kitchen once, as I thought this was what a college student was supposed to eat. I made do.

I'd been spooked walking down Arthur Avenue in my first weeks on campus, trying to get to a market where I could buy cereal and red-capped whole milk. The old Italian shops hung animal carcasses in the windows—I never looked long enough to discern which animals. All I knew was that I wanted to avoid seeing them, and thus I avoided really appreciating that I lived in one of the great historic culinary neighborhoods of New York City. I was seventeen when I moved into the dorm, and I wasn't ready, despite all my bluster, to be on my own. Making friends in high school had been easy enough because I was in orchestra: They came ready-made, like the fresh rosin in a new case. Though at home, I never wanted to upset my father, I had been accustomed to being confident in who I was if shy when I was in the world. Suddenly, that magic in me had vanished, and I didn't know where to seek the support that would help me along. If I'd been at the Lincoln Center campus in Manhattan, I'd be fine, I told my mom. The room and board there was much higher in price, though, and my grant and student loans were tapped out; my family's contribution was already assumed to be more than we could afford.

I would go home every weekend to see Todd—but really to escape the new reality of the campus that I couldn't find my place in. He kept living at home to go to a local state school and study computer science, and a lot of my best friends from high school were also still there. At college, in the dorm, I'd struggled with a sudden and intense social anxiety, as well as a fear of alcohol—and whatever loss of control might ensue in drinking it, whatever bad thing inside me that nuns and my dad were convinced was there, that I too feared because I knew addiction was in my family, might be released—that made me reclusive. I'd press play on my portable CD player right before opening the door to my room, usually listening to the Mars Volta's *De-Loused in the Comatorium* at an ear-drum-piercing volume, and not hit stop until I was in my seat in class, the professor already giving their lecture.

My second year, I moved back home and started commuting: I'd done a sneaky internal transfer to Lincoln Center, which backfired once I saw the bill for housing. Though I'd never known the particulars of the household finances—I went to Catholic school and we drank whole milk, but we didn't go skiing or on any vacations that weren't to visit my aunt and uncle in Florida—I assumed college would be taken care of. Then, my dad lost his job. A little work-study gig for spending cash wasn't going to cut it anymore: I now needed to work to pay for a car, my train tickets, and everything else I might want. This was fine for me in that I could hide my intense anxiety behind work and commuting; I could blame them for why I wasn't making new friends or seeking out those new opportunities I'd always believed were the key to unlocking my future. (I also found out that internships were unpaid, and my parents rightfully scoffed when I suggested I could learn by working for free at a record label or radio station.) I found solace as I always did, in listening to music, reading novels, and being social on the internet, and I burrowed myself ever more deeply into this relationship, not knowing how I could ever find love again if I was so afraid of talking to new people.

—

In the story I want to tell about this eleven-year relationship, in the story that I've passed like flour through a sifter to perfect as a tidy explanation of why I didn't have the youth of my dreams, we just got caught up in the momentum of our relationship and were good at living separate lives together. There's truth in that.

There's also truth in him suggesting I stop eating when I was enjoying a chimichanga-style burrito too much for his liking; there was him telling me I'd gained too much weight after freshman year of college. His fucked-up comments should've been the end of things. But I didn't know what a good relationship looked like or could be: I knew that I was afraid of not having a refuge from the strain my dad's job loss was putting on my parents' marriage, from the stress of a family house where I didn't feel allowed to grow into an adult, even if the refuge itself often proved to be unpleasant. This unpleasantness had a tinge of romance to it, at least, in the push-pull and dramas I would perform. He refused to go to trivia, and I threw a full water bottle through my own car's passenger window, the frustration building because he refused to go anywhere, have any fun. How was my refuge also strangling me, also keeping me from becoming anything at all that I'd hoped to be? I retaliated in other ways, too, by entertaining a co-worker's crush on me, someone impressed by me as the first person he'd ever known who wore a scarf—Long Island, where the bar for difference rarely rises from the sand.

I felt unseen, too demanding; I wish I'd known how common this dynamic was, the constantly being told I was *too much*—asking too much, demanding too much, wanting too much. I didn't know; I thought I was uniquely broken, that I had no choice but to hold on to whatever was being offered to me because I was strange and reclusive and afraid of myself because everyone kept telling me I needed to be, at threat of violence or rejection or eternal damnation. Because when push came to shove, I did throw a water bottle through a window rather than say, "You know what? This is over." We were two young adult children of young parents, dealing with our damage.

How the mighty girl-king had fallen! I was subsisting on Starbucks lemon loaf and yogurt parfaits, because I worked there and got a 30 percent discount, as well as Snickers bars and Red Bull to get my schoolwork done. Between that job and doing web design for wacky local egomaniacs found on Craigslist, I'd be sugar and caffeine loaded in the library, writing about just war theory, Walter Benjamin, and eighteenth-century English poetry. During an oral exam, my critical theory professor told me to slow down: "You are speaking with the cadence of someone who's very tired," she said, and I almost cried at the very idea that anyone would notice. I'd taken to drinking a double tall soy mocha latte on my way to school, this mix of espresso and chocolate a smooth means of caffeinating myself, and the soy milk chosen because of an emergent lactose intolerance; I'd eat it with a pain au chocolat, and its butter-laden laminated dough would negate the good choice of soy. Chocolate, caffeine, Pepto-Bismol, and Excedrin—these were how I made it through.

I graduated from college in 2007, and I resented the questionnaires asking us where we were planning to work. In the lines reserved for an answer, I wrote that I already had a job as a barista.

—

College, while tumultuous because of money troubles and commuting, had been a time that fostered and gave shape to that lifetime "progressive" streak. I'd always been attracted to anything that connoted "left-wing"; here I learned what that actually meant through a contemporary philosophy class taught by an ex-Jesuit Marxist. He told graduate students that their democratic socialism was a cop-out; he told us undergraduates that most of us were only there to line the coffers of the university and were meant for middle management. On the door to his office, he had a sign that said, "My salary is $110,000 per year. Make me earn it." Everything he said and made us read, like Herbert Marcuse's *One-Dimensional Man*, made me uncomfortable, made me squirm in my seat: This class didn't show me that what I'd always experienced was common to my gender, like one about feminism and American poetry; it made me grapple with everything I'd ever been taught to value. I probably got a B+; I was always getting a B+. But it was that Marxist philosophy professor whose inspiration I was harnessing when I wrote "barista" on a line meant for my career plans. After all, taking philosophy classes and working at a corporate coffee shop had equal influence on me and my perception of the world—its imbalance, its inequity. Without both, the fair-trade chocolate label never would've registered in my mind.

I'd been changed by classes, taught to read and to think critically about my unchecked preferences, biases, and concerns, but I'd also been changed by my thrust into wage labor, into being treated as garbage by strangers and the camaraderie that emerges among workers. All of this laid the foundation for me to figure out how to align my actions with my beliefs. Did I think it would come in the form of food? It would take some time before the chocolate bar labels would open a portal to a new life, but this accumulation of knowledge, taste, and instinct was pointing me toward something. In hindsight, this accumulation is key to my becoming; at the time, it felt like I was feeling around in the dark for meaning.

—

My mom was always worried that by staying with Todd, I was going to make the same mistakes she had made by getting married young and having me at twenty-two. But I had no interest in marriage or kids, just a desire to be comfortable enough to start writing book reviews and get myself a magazine job eventually. I had dug my heels in with this relationship and I didn't know how to undo it, or whether I was ready to. I'd envisioned an easier transition into adult life, but I was thwarted by money at every turn. There was never enough of it. I still needed that escape hatch. Survival meant coping with misery and creating my own world out of spite.

The first office job I'd gotten after college fired me at the end of the summer, 2009, and because of the financial crisis, I was able to use this opportunity to defer my student loans without much question. Everyone assumed I'd been laid off and gave me sympathy. I sat in my childhood bedroom, which I'd haphazardly painted lime green when I was nineteen, and applied for job after job at literary agencies, book publishers, and magazines. I received one bite, and it was from the senior digital copy editor at *New York* magazine: Would I want to come in for a copy test?

Despite everything that had been going on with my parents' divorce, I hadn't completely given up on myself and my magazine dreams. I'd been blogging on my own website and writing book reviews (for free) for any publication that would have me. At every opportunity, I took the train into the city to go to readings and literary events, trying to will myself into a new life. Giving in to the crappy job and suburban life wasn't an option, and this email confirmed that perhaps I wasn't doomed.

I put on a black blazer and some Michael Kors heels of my mother's that I could barely walk in, and I took the train to Penn Station and the 1 train down to Canal Street. I'd known already from a Google search that the person hiring had gone to Harvard, and I was nervous. The test was just a few paragraphs of old copy, and I used the copyediting symbols I'd learned from one two-hour class and the internet to make my corrections. When I followed up a week later, I was told that I did well and could come in for a shift—from 8:40 a.m. to 6:30 p.m. I briefly questioned the legality of this but knew I had no choice, and I showed up for my first day. Within hours, I was asked whether I wanted a full-time job, because apparently I was fast and good at this: My excessive internet addiction and spending all my free time reading was apparently finally going to pay off. I was hired around Christmas, and in January, I was moving out—and in with Todd.

That first apartment in Huntington Village, on the north shore of Long Island, was the upstairs of a house owned by a young married couple. The husband was a contractor, and his renovation gave me the new place of my dreams: exposed brick, wood floors, and lots of natural light. We split the $1,200 rent down the middle. I was working mainly from home for the magazine, still on those ten-hour shifts that didn't build in either a lunch break or time to go to the bathroom, but I felt lucky to have the job at all and not to be paying a few hundred extra dollars a month for an LIRR ticket. Who was I to question that I had to go to the toilet with my laptop? I'd never done an internship; I'd never paid the dues.

What I could do while I was working these long shifts

during which I couldn't leave my laptop was try to make this first tiny kitchen my own. It took up a corner of the room that also included the dining room table and living room couch. Prophetically, a copy of Molly O'Neill's *American Food Writing: An Anthology* was set upon the cabinets. On the freezer, I'd taped a promotional bookmark for Douglas Coupland's *All Families Are Psychotic* to remind myself of just that. I didn't know what I was building in my life, but knew that this was a first step toward what I had imagined for myself. It would just take me longer to get there: no ski trip money, no internships, just extreme dedication to making myself someone of whom I could be proud. First, I'd have to learn how to grocery shop.

Todd had been the one cooking at first, making the same basic dinners his mother had made because he didn't have an adventurous nor curious palate: breaded and fried chicken cutlets, the canned green beans, Swedish meatballs with rice noodles, Hamburger Helper (his family also introduced me to this, which I found to be delicious and unfairly maligned). But he had started to go on work trips that allowed me the space to finally try out a long nagging interest in being vegetarian that had only grown as I was religiously going to hot yoga classes where being vegan was discussed as the pinnacle of human achievement. I started to learn how to roast vegetables and cook meaty portobello mushrooms. This initial interest, this difference I was cultivating between us when it came to dinner, was the first rupture that showed we couldn't go on together forever. This difference, though, was care for myself: for what I was eating, how it felt in my body, and how it aligned with the life I wanted to live. If I were to deny this, I would be denying any chance of living a life I actually liked. I felt this in my bones: a need to claim cooking as care for the planet, but I had to claim it as caring for myself first.

Whereas in Patchogue there was no bodega at the corner to run to for a Hershey's bar, in Huntington Village, there was a whole natural foods supermarket called Wild by Nature that was just up the street. I would spend my free time there or at the local indie bookstore, Book Revue, where I was able to fill out my shelves with discounted remainders of all the books I hadn't gotten to in college and support my nascent interest (thanks to the boom of translation inspired by Roberto Bolaño's success) in Latin American literature. My life became the grocery store and the bookstore, the coffee shop and the indie movie theater—as I'd wanted, in a way, just out in a liberal pocket of Long Island and not the East Village.

Having this access to a natural grocer after spending much of my college years eating as cheaply as I possibly could out of the Columbus Circle Whole Foods hot bar meant I was browsing labels and finding out about "organic" and that chocolate-favorite, "fair trade." I realized bananas, too, would come with fair-trade stickers, and so did sugar. Coffee, too! I put it together that what was grown far away, in tropical climates where labor could be exploited, required an extra level of certainty that these items might be okay to buy. I became a bit fanatical about organic and fair trade;

when I gave up meat for good in 2011 but would still pick up chicken and eggs for Todd, I made sure it had all the markings of chickens that might have enjoyed their life right up until their demise: cage-free, organic, humane.

I was learning my way around the natural grocery store and cooking simply, but what really caught my interest was baking. It had always been the only cooking I liked to get into the kitchen for, and I'd imagined those catered dinner parties as a kid where I'd impress with a dessert, some towering Victoria sponge or caramel-soaked flan or chocolate ganache tart. The frivolity of dessert, of the sweet finish, removed the sense of duty that loomed over savory cooking.

Chocolate was the easiest switch to make, along with bananas and sugar. The internet told me that white Domino sugar was given that color and fine grind through the use of bone char: Cattle bones are burned and the activated carbon is what filters the color from the crystals. Bananas, I read, when they're grown with chemical pesticides, expose laborers to toxins; fair-trade organically grown trees, I read, ensure better working conditions. Chocolate, I could swear, tasted better if I knew where it came from, and I loved discerning new notes in every bar; this gave me ever more varieties to try. There was stone-ground Mexican chocolate, big baking rounds of chocolate from TCHO, unroasted chocolate from Raaka—looking for the fair-trade label became a way of tasting more variety than I would ever get from my once-beloved Snickers.

—

What I didn't realize then, and would come to gradually know, is that these labels obscure quite a bit. They can be a way of assuaging first-world guilt over consuming commodities whose trade has long moved along colonial routes. The label can serve as a Band-Aid over the open wounds of economic and political imperialism that still reverberate in the relations between Europe and the U.S. and Latin America and Africa. Organic certifications are pricey to access and often don't take a farm's entire processes into account; for smaller farmers in regions susceptible to climate change and ever more invasive pests, not relying on pesticide can mean no crops to sell at all. One never knows the conditions unless one is at the farm itself, and that doesn't just apply to agriculture outside the U.S., but within it as well. This reality of invisible labor and the demand for cheap commodities means there are very few incentives to do things "right," whatever "right" may be in a specific context.

Whether these labels have a real impact on the living and economic conditions at the source also didn't occur to me until much later. In the meantime, I had begun to obsessively bake, inspired by the fact that I didn't know where to get a vegan cookie made with fair-trade chocolate and sugar, New York state flour, and organic ingredients, and I wanted to eat one. The first thing I ever made vegan that impressed people I knew was a chocolate-chunk cookie: chewy from the combination of molasses-rich dark brown sugar and beige crystals of cane sugar, and fatty from a blend of coconut oil and coconut milk that I made as a baking fat to use in lieu of butter or margarines I found unpleasant on the tongue.

We'd moved by 2012 into a new apartment that was still in Huntington Village: this one with two bedrooms, one for an office, and a kitchen that was a room of its own. In my memory, it is huge. It was in this kitchen—my first important, real kitchen—that I became a baker, with a metal and wood rack to hold the lime green (a theme of my youthful taste) KitchenAid stand mixer that I'd bought for myself, taking a stand against the assumption that I should wait to receive one as a wedding gift. Every day, while I worked and while I didn't, I got into that kitchen and experimented with headphones in and my iPod playing Nada Surf's discography on shuffle. Birthday cakes, cupcakes, brownies, and cookies. I learned how to bake traditionally and then applied my understandings to vegan ingredients: flaxseed meal mixed with water became egg; almonds blended with water became milk; and canned full-fat coconut milk became heavy cream. At five a.m., I'd get up and bake. At seven a.m., I'd go to hot yoga. At 8:40 a.m., I'd log on to work. Every day.

I'd decided to try my baking fat and all my accumulated organic baking ingredients in a cookie I'd already made the "traditional" way, from a cookbook by chef Thomas Keller called *Ad Hoc at Home*. It was the first cookbook of my adult life, a housewarming gift of sorts from Kerry and her then-boyfriend. Through copyediting the restaurant coverage at the magazine, I was also learning all the names of big chefs and restaurants; I was understanding how "cool" was manufactured from the inside, and from what I could tell, the people who called the shots liked Keller. From this book, I'd learn a lot of the basics and I'd make brownies so filled with butter that they were, truly, a motivating factor in my finally giving up dairy after years of clues that I was lactose intolerant. When I wanted a cookie, I wanted *this book*'s chocolate chip cookie, which had struck me as perfect for its chew: It didn't crumble, and it wasn't overly soft.

I put my chilled coconut fat in the bowl of the mixer, and let it be beaten by the paddle attachment. I added the other half of chilled fat and the sugar, and to my joy, it began to cream to a sandy base, just like butter would. Then, in three parts, I poured in all my dry ingredients—the flour, the baking soda, the kosher salt, the cornstarch I was trying out as an egg replacement to bind the dough—and it was coming together, but not quite correctly. It was pebbly and not forming a ball around the paddle, as it should have. I thought quickly about what was missing, and—aha! It would be moisture from the eggs that was lacking. I remembered that a large egg is two ounces of liquid, about a quarter cup, and so I poured in half a cup of almond milk. The dough formed around the paddle. I added my chocolate chunks, which I'd hand-chopped, and the cookie was born. I chilled it, then formed the dough into balls, and baked for twelve minutes on unbleached parchment paper, turning halfway through.

A friend from yoga came by at my invitation to pick some up, a first taste-tester, and she couldn't believe they were vegan. Even Todd, so far not very motivated to support my obsessive baking endeavors nor my veganism, was impressed. That friend and others from the yoga studio, which is where I'd drop off my excess recipe tests, started to ask me to bake for their events and birthdays. La Pirata Kitchen was born—the pirate kitchen, run illegally from our apartment. A man got on a mic at the New York City Vegan Drinks meetup I'd catered and said, "I've been vegan for twenty years, and these are the best chocolate chip cookies I've ever had." My linzer cookies were renowned by bloggers. A local paper called me the "Non-Dairy Queen."

I was still working as a copy editor for the magazine—I'd gradually won some small victories when I became the senior editor, such as lunch breaks and eight-hour workdays—and running the microbakery on the side. From the first order of 200 cupcakes in July 2012 through August of the next year, I took on a wholesale client, baked countless birthday cakes, and sold cupcakes and cookies at farmers' markets. My workdays could stretch to twenty hours long, but it never felt that way. I'd bake for a morning delivery and then make buns, veggie burgers, and doughnuts from scratch for friends. I'd send out cakes and come home to work on whatever molecular pet obsession I had that week. When I went to Book Revue now, it wasn't to find literary fiction, but cookbooks of every sort. I was constantly thinking about new packaging, new ingredients, new cookies. "You've become compulsively creative," Todd said to me one day while changing the CD in his car. It wasn't said with a positive tone. My obsession was stretching the limits of our reality: We had been two teenage weirdos when we had met, clinging to each other. Did we actually need each other anymore?

At the farmers' markets during the summer of 2013, I was meeting folks who weren't coming to the culinary realm out of some dedication to Escoffier's brigades and cutting teeth as line cooks doing brunch shifts. They were in the dirt, and I traded explanations of the ratios for the coconut oil butter I was making for insight into how they were growing carrots and what I should do with the frizzled green tops. I wasn't a cool person in the city food world, maybe, but I could be a person who gave a shit. This was where I learned every land gives food of some sort; every land provides a culture—even Long Island's.

I was becoming rooted to land I had thought of as barren, as fruitless—land that could never give me culture, which I would have to seek out elsewhere. But here was this land, showing off its fruits each week to me: People who not only cared about the terroir, but who also had their hands in the dirt. This turned me toward savory cooking in a whole new way, making it just as compelling as the sweet. I'd learned how to feed and care for myself simply with roasted vegetables and breaded mushrooms, but when I cooked the food of my home—roasted its purple potatoes, snapped its fresh spring peas, and salted its summer tomatoes—it forged a way of cooking for me that was as rooted as my baking in choices made for the sake of soil, for the good of workers. Here was my childlike delight in simple pleasures, renewed.

Local, seasonal, fair trade never felt like complicated or difficult choices to make: They were just the right ones.

—

As food became my life, Todd and I drifted apart. Living separate lives together no longer really made sense, and we'd begun fighting once I went vegan, once we were eating different meals. Eleven years to the day of the first date we went on to see that community production of *The Music Man*, we broke up. He'd been acting strangely, avoidant, and one night while I was brushing my teeth, I shouted to the other room, "Are we breaking up or what?" Finally, the answer was yes. I couldn't sleep out of anxiety, but I knew it was the right move, even if it would be painful. I made one last cake for the microbakery, whisking batter while feeling like I could faint from the shock. I'd long wondered who would be there to catch me if this relationship ended, and now I'd be finding out that it was every friend who'd always been there. On Doug's rooftop in Bushwick, two days after the breakup, I drank wine with him, Kerry, Justin, and Luke, who I'd known since we were teenagers, even before Todd. They were there to pick me up, and I wish I'd realized they would've always been there sooner. But maybe this was the right timing; maybe I just needed to learn that I could make the best vegan chocolate chip cookies anyone has ever had—then I could be free. "Get Lucky" by Daft Punk came on the stereo, and we all wordlessly got up, dancing ourselves back downstairs to clean up, and I knew

I'd be okay—and that I'd be moving to Brooklyn. It wasn't a conscious choice, nothing I could labor over or debate with a list of pros and cons: Again, the truth was in my bones. It just took a really long time on occasion to make itself known, or was it me taking a long time to notice?

Todd and I had become comfortable enough as individuals, as people, to no longer need the escape hatch. It was never a relationship for life, but it was a relationship that anchored me while I became the very different person I was always going to be. What it did was provide a container, a safer space, to grow within. Closing the microbakery made sense because of the move, because it was exhausting me and not really making any money despite consistent sales. I thought it was the end of the clearest dream I'd ever had, but it was the beginning of my life—the first time I'd learn that a life could have as many beginnings as it needed, that nothing had to be linear. Nothing could be. It just accumulates.

The most telling thing for me in hindsight is how much I remember of those years was me creating myself, especially when I started to go to yoga, became obsessed with food as a cook rather than just an eater, got into veganism, and was reading as much as I possibly could. I was going to see movies at the Cinema Arts Centre regularly, alone. What this time in my twenties gave me was a space away from my parents while they were getting divorced to figure out who I could be without the pressure and diversion of school. A lot of it was a way of coping, sure—not just with my family life imploding but also with a boyfriend who made no effort. These were years of self-directed unschooling, revealing to me that while I had thought my life was taking me in the direction of the literary world, it was food that was opening me up and quelling that long-debilitating social anxiety. At farmers' markets and through selling birthday cakes to the few vegans on Long Island, I was meeting people who were interested in things that I cared about, who knew things I didn't yet. Having the foundation of food made me less nervous in conversations. At the stand mixer, I found my voice. Chocolate was my portal into noticing that food came from somewhere, that there was a story of it before it ever turned into what we eat.

After closing down La Pirata Kitchen and moving to Bushwick, Brooklyn—finally, at twenty-seven, really doing the reverse migration to the city I'd always longed for—I decided that I could combine food and magazine work by writing about food. In a very on-the-nose way, my first story was a profile of the vegan chocolatier Lagusta Yearwood, whose blog on the ethics of eating and science of recipes I'd read like a great novel. She had a chocolate shop in New Paltz, New York, that I'd made a pilgrimage to once with a friend for an intimate savory tasting menu. Her chocolates and perspective shaped my own.

But it wasn't just literal chocolate that was defining my way of writing about food; it was everything that chocolate had taught me about how food comes to our hands, especially in the affluent global north. As with the sugar, bananas, and coffee—and coffee, chocolate, and bananas are great intercrops, helping one another grow when planted in the same soil—it was all changing my relationship to what I ate, and thus what I wanted to write about. While I'd spent so much of my life thus far longing for certain flavors, now I also wanted those flavors to be not just delicious, but also represent a care for the earth, those who labor for it, and those animals who also add to its richness. I'd gone from feminism meaning I would eat a steak to show *the man* that a woman had a legitimate appetite to only eating fair-trade chocolate for reasons that, frankly, weren't too dissimilar. Eating marked a path toward if not freedom for me—freedom maybe was no longer my idealistic goal—then maybe something like harmony. To use a seventies term, my consciousness had been raised and there was no way to turn back.

—

Even in the nineteenth century, in advertisements for chocolate, the cacao pod itself had been drawn in. Getting rid of the pod meant people forgot that it came from a tree: Chocolate could be magic, and if it were magic, no one had to worry about who was at the source and whether or not they were being paid. How much food has mirrored this advertising strategy? The pretend magic obscuring reality keeps it cheap; because it's cheap, people eat a ton of it; and because it's so common and cheap, the insurgence of craft chocolate is nothing but a drop in the bucket of multinational corporations. A tiny, tiny, tiny drop that is carrying the bulk of the weight for undoing the sins of Hershey's—which bought

Scharffen Berger, understood as the first U.S. craft chocolate company, in 2005—and other massive industrial chocolate producers. The FDA only requires a bar to contain 10 percent cacao; much of what's available in any major supermarket is barely going to surpass that. Though large industrial chocolate-makers promise that they will move toward ethical labor practices and ecologically sustainable growing, there has been little proof of a real commitment. Why would they? Chocolate, even when it's only made with 10 percent cacao, still sells, and craft chocolate can't compete.

This is why chocolate is both so dangerous and so filled with potential to change how more people think about food: It's a formative flavor, something we're introduced to as children, something we're taught is a reward, a treat, a sign that we're on the right track in life—that we are loved. Was I satisfied, as a kid, by dancing onstage or playing the violin as acts on their own, or did I enjoy them more because I knew the gold box of Godiva would be mine once I saw my grandpa in the hallway of the auditorium? Had I not been set up to see chocolate as something that spoke to both my palate and my delight in being appreciated for my performances, would it have also been the food that opened me up to an inequitable, destructive food system? It could be that more folks could be opened up to these realities through chocolate, precisely because of the role it plays in our hearts, our nostalgia. Nostalgia is such a powerful force when it comes to food. It drives our choices regularly. So is comfort, and there are few things more comforting than a slice of chocolate cake or a bowl of chocolate ice cream. In its sinister corporate underpinnings lies the potential for transformation.

Longing for both chocolate and calm made my life change directions in ways that I could not have foreseen, and through the former, I made an escape into a life that wasn't precisely what I'd hoped for, but gave me the space to get ready for what I did want. Now in my late twenties, I was safe enough to be myself: Following my curiosity and my taste had brought me thrills and opportunities. I started to eat different chocolate because I preferred to think my joy wasn't at the cost of someone else's; I continued because I was hungry for the variety, the experience of learning what I liked—chocolate, as diverse as the array of apples. This had been hidden from me.

These more highfalutin reasons had their purposes, but in my palate and intellectual transformation, I was also looking for a cleanse—a means of shedding an old, ill-fitting skin to enable the good girl I'd been to turn into a woman, autonomous. But it would always be harder than I thought to get free.

On Lamb

A LIGHT MANIA BEFELL ME IN THE AFTERMATH OF THAT long-term relationship. "Manic hubris," I called it. It was the manic hubris that made me start buying crop tops from American Apparel; the manic hubris that made me use Tinder like a video game. My debut into Brooklyn womanhood at twenty-seven in August of 2013 found me ravenous, enraptured by possibility, almost teenage again with friends sleeping over in my queen-size mattress on the floor or beside it on my thick purple yoga mat.

My books were stacked against the walls; a mantel from a closed-off fireplace held a flea market Virgen de Guadalupe print given to me by my cousin Emma and a framed poster of my favorite movie, *Before Night Falls*. If I'd spent my Huntington years getting more deeply acquainted with the contemporary literary canon, both in English and in translation, now I was obsessed with women and anyone who queered expectation: *I Love Dick* by Chris Kraus; *Heroines* by Kate Zambreno; *Inferno (A Poet's Novel)* by Eileen Myles; *How Should a Person Be?* by Sheila Heti. I spent all my time and money when I wasn't eating or working trawling all the city's indie bookstores, looking for new women to read. I'd found out that I was one in a long line of us who'd been told they were too much, who were treated poorly for bursting at the seams and needing more, who were told something bad and dark was lurking inside them. I underlined and filled the margins with my notes, my recognitions; in *Heroines*, I listed all the physical ailments I'd suffered in my last relationship—knee pain, diarrhea, constant crying—as though I could finally see and admit the minor horrors of it. I wanted to know everyone who came before and to discover what they could tell me about myself.

I moved into a large upstairs room in a duplex off the Halsey Street L, which was what people referred to as "deep Bushwick," so far from the gentrified core of Williamsburg that just walking a few blocks had me crossing the imaginary line into Queens. It cost $800 per month and I had four roommates, but I only shared a bathroom with two of them. The kitchen was teeny-tiny, an Ikea table one could stand at and folded in when not in use was the only dining area, so I ate meals on my floor, at my desk, on the front stoop: apples cut up into chunks stirred into oats, topped with a healthy spoonful of peanut butter and a sprinkle of cinnamon for breakfast; some thoughtless desk salad for lunch; a trip out into the city for dinner.

I discovered a new love for eating by myself, trained as I

was by my time going to the movies alone. The movies were dark places, though. Learning how to go out to eat without company felt bigger, and I took a long walk to the subway one day to finally try MOB's, a vegan restaurant that used to be on Atlantic Avenue. I wanted to try their veggie burger with housemade cashew cheese. When I arrived and asked for a seat, I was nervous, anticipating judgment, but no one seemed to notice or care. Now that I was in the city, my heart more broken by the end of the bakery than the end of my eleven-year-long relationship, I was able to eat all the foods all the time that I ever read about: There were jackfruit chimichangas and every single possible vegan burger. There were tempeh Buffalo wings that I ate alone at the counter at Champs Diner; tofu bánh mì for lunch from Falansai; teff-flour injera topped with beets, lentils, and kale at Bunna. It was a vegan's haven, and now there was no stick-in-the-mud boyfriend getting in my way. The feeling of not having to perform, not having to care about someone else's mood or how much they were liking their meal—I could never tire of it, of the release it provides.

I could've been sad. I could've been a lamb to the slaughter of single city life at the dawn of the dating apps. Instead, I was in my glory. Though every phone call from someone who wanted to order a birthday cake was like a knife to the chest, it was clear that trading a stand mixer for tight dresses and indie pop parties that started at midnight was what I needed.

—

It was also time to focus on making a serious foray into food writing. My accidental experience of running a small artisanal food business coincided with food taking up a whole new role in the broader cultural realm. This space seemed tailor-made for the girl I had been and not the woman I was becoming, who wanted her eating to in some way match up with an ethical commitment to land, workers, and animals. I was buying *Saveur* and *Bon Appétit* and *Food & Wine*, wondering where I fit into the whole thing. If my icons were becoming vegan chocolatier Lagusta Yearwood and cookbook author Isa Chandra Moskowitz, could I ever hope to enter the pages of the major food magazines?

Every culinary icon of the time, whether Anthony Bourdain or David Chang or their magazine *Lucky Peach*, was adamant that vegans and vegetarians were not welcome, could never know a good meal. This anxiety became my own, despite my reality: Becoming vegan was making my world make sense; it was showing me there is life, there are hands, at every point in the food system. The first three issues of that cult magazine all had dead animals on the cover; on the fourth, a living cow—an herbivorous creature—tagged on its ear as livestock, is being offered a hot dog. All the regular food magazines, too, had roasted birds and grilled steaks on their covers. The women in culture who occupied less restaurant-obsessed space and focused on home cooking didn't offer much in the way of options, either. Their appetites were understood to include what was approved by Bourdain and Chang; a notion of good eating that didn't prioritize animal products was some California idea they couldn't wrap their heads around, and it was their heads that food media revolved around.

I could find much more to identify with in the domestic writing of women, though; that's true. All my life I'd avoided the notion that there was anything for me in the kitchen unless it had the impressive tenor of a chef's feat, a display of prowess and free time rather than love and care. If I wasn't figuring out how to use some basic science and math to perfectly calibrate a vegan chocolate-chunk cookie, I didn't deem it a worthy endeavor. It seemed to me there wasn't a place anywhere for a vegan.

This conundrum always brought me back to cracking open the colorful seventies tome *No More Masks! An Anthology of Twentieth-Century American Women Poets* in my college feminist poetry class. These poems—they shook me awake to the double binds and let me know there was no escaping patriarchy, and though I thought I was doing my best to act against and as though feminism were a given didn't change a damn thing on any structural level. I could yell, *I REFUSE TO LET MY GENDER DEFINE ME; I WILL EAT THE STEAK-FRITES* over and over—it didn't matter. A trap had been set, and it turned out that I wasn't like professional women chefs who overstated their commitment to cooking meat and innards, so certainly I couldn't be Bourdain or Chang: I felt something about the dead animals serving as food. They weren't mere props to show I could be just like one of the boys or sexy even while fulfilling my hunger for flesh. I knew they were alive, and I wanted to stop eating them.

Every step of the way, it seemed, every choice I made as a woman brought me to a new dichotomy that felt like a trap, and indeed, there seemed to be two ways for women in food: the sexpot or "one of the boys." Both ways included meat.

"I have nothing to declare but my greed," writes Nigella Lawson on the very first page *How to Eat: The Pleasures and Principles of Good Food*. Me neither. But when one writes something like that, it is easily understood to mean that she eats *everything*. That book, her first, came out in the year 2000. Lawson would become famous for being a woman with an appetite, one she claimed and indulged repeatedly in cookbooks and on television shows. Women were accepted more in the food world, this was clear, if they adopted the masculine posture of the ruthless omnivore, ready to eat anything but ideally a large piece of animal meat on a bone. A chef like Angie Mar did photo shoots in elaborate gowns, bared cleavage, a plate of meat in front of her with the whole bottle of red wine. Her gowns, pink; the meat, dripping with a feral red. *Ordering the steak doesn't make a woman less feminine*, these images seemed to say. If anything, it seemed to play it up—to suggest an anything-goes approach to an appetite for food seems to be interpreted as veiled sexual desire and availability. Though depicted eating and enjoying food, women with an acceptable voluptuousness were also chiefly in the business of cooking and serving meals up: a sprinkle of subversion on a rotten old dish of servicing the men at the table.

The glamour and sex appeal she and Lawson exuded was in contrast to how other lauded women in food were positioned, those who weren't appealing to the men but still mapped its stereotypical appetite onto their approach: Gabrielle Hamilton ran Prune in New York City, where pink also reigned as the color of choice, but her memoir was titled *Blood, Bones, and Butter* and she never lacked for these on the menu. April Bloomfield, who revamped pub fare at the Spotted Pig, was pictured on the cover of her first cookbook, *A Girl and Her Pig*, with a dead one around her shoulders—while the title on its own evoked a touching tale of young woman and pet, the image ensured no confusion that this was about showing a girl (though, in this case, Bloomfield was clearly a woman) could also feel nothing when confronted with dead animals. This would always be the ticket to the boys' club of the food world, and I would never gain admission. But I could tell there had to be another way.

My appetite had so long been defined by its eager taste for lamb chops, lobster, steak, and salty prosciutto—now it swung wholly toward plants. Surviving my parents' tumultuous divorce and the end of a long relationship that defined and constrained so much of my young life showed me that I could withstand a lot more than I'd given myself credit for: I could muscle through this perceived barrier, too.

—

The only meat I've ever cooked is lamb. It was the formative meat for me, the meat of my first memory, and I was always ravenous for it—ravenous in a race at dinners in childhood against my brother to see who could collect more bones from the chops onto their plate. I wanted to surprise my mom on her birthday when I was sixteen (she'd be turning thirty-eight) so I looked up an Ina Garten leg of lamb recipe that had me stuffing the flesh with cloves of garlic and rubbing it in yogurt. This was a strange choice for a first-time cook: I only ever got in the kitchen to feed myself and my brother blown-out microwaved hot dogs and Ellio's frozen pizzas and frozen raviolis served with nothing during our summers in the house by ourselves. But I wanted to do something nice for my mom, who was always doing everything for us, and so I stepped into the kitchen.

It was also a strange choice because we never ate yogurt in our house—too hippie-dippy to have ever crossed the threshold—and though the rest of us loved eating Greek food from the Old Olive Tree on Main Street, it was the only food that ever gave my mother food poisoning. Because she was never able to rest or be sick (who would've taken care of the kids? Who would've cooked the meals?), this bout with food poisoning was terrifying and memorable for its rarity. She had to sleep in my brother's room, which was slightly closer to the bathroom, and crawled herself to the toilet to vomit while my baby sister was always close on her tail. But on the internet of the early 2000s, this was the Barefoot Contessa lamb recipe I could find, and so this was the one I cooked. It wasn't greeted with applause. I went back to cooking only what could go in the microwave.

My mom recalls it as delicious: "I truly appreciated someone cooking for me and you were so excited to do it." If I remember it as going over poorly, she says, it's because my brother probably mocked me—"anything for a laugh." I want to ask him, desperately; I want all my memories that he took with him back.

The other time I cooked a leg of lamb was for Easter the year I was transitioning to veganism. It would be a last hurrah of my favorite meat, of buttery biscuits. I had been making the switch but also learning about nutrition in the wake of a back injury that wasn't healing; I realized I hadn't been eating enough—it wasn't enough to have just a green juice when you went to hot yoga and on a 2.5-mile hike, apparently, and my lunches of steamed kale, brown rice, and a couple of tablespoons of beans weren't cutting it either—and was dipping in and out of the diet while I healed. This was in Huntington Village, and I went to the butcher counter at Wild By Nature, where I purchased a seventy-five-dollar organic, grass-fed leg of lamb imported from New Zealand and prepared it for family. Everyone preferred the biscuits, proving my natural talents lay with flour, not flesh.

—

Lamb was the meat I loved, the only meat I prepared, but it is a meat of a loss of innocence. I think of Catholic Mass, of Jesus as the lamb of God who takes away the sins of the world (have mercy on us). I think of paintings of Jesus holding a lamb—who does that lamb represent? It bleeds in Jesus's arms, harkening back to his own crucifixion, his own taking on of our sins, and is an image from the Book of Revelation, about when Jesus returns to bring us all to heaven (or send us to hell). He is the lamb; he shows us the lamb.

A lamb is a symbol of purity and innocence, a lamb is "sacrificial." Its death is meaningful for what it represents, not as a death unto itself. A lamb is a baby sheep. It is one of the few animals killed for food who retains its name in death and life: Is this a sign of respect or its opposite? The meat of a full-grown sheep is mutton, which doesn't have the same cachet, the same culinary ring to it as *lamb*. There's nothing sacrificed, nothing gained, through the death of an old sheep. A lamb, though, doesn't have to die. Is that why it tastes so good?

And how does it taste? Why was it so delicious to me from the beginning? I have my memories of its flavor, of how it was different from steak or pork or chicken—more special. Could I eat it now, in secret, for a reminder? Yes, but it wouldn't taste the same to me as it had when I was a child anyway; it would be inseparable from the life taken. To eat lamb now would feel grotesque, cannibalistic. I think about it and feel nausea. Far, far away from the joy and hunger of me as gluttonous toddler, competitive teenager collecting bones, young adult playing the part of hopeful gourmand, stuffing her seventy-five-dollar meat with garlic cloves. So I google, "what does lamb taste like," and I see it described as gamey with a hint of sweetness; firm, yet tender. Most lamb is "grass-finished," they say, as though describing a pot that's been given a glaze, but American lamb can be "grain-finished," which might cut the earthiness to soothe a palate reared on industrial beef and chicken.

I loved the lamb chops most of all, the racks, with the bones right there. You could collect the bones, as my brother and I did, to see who ate more; this might be why I'm now, as my mom says, "the Rain Man of oysters"—I always know how many everyone at the table has eaten, without consciously paying attention. They were red and tender, and I read now that they have a lot of fat, which might have accounted for my preference. I've always loved fat, the fattier the better.

When lamb was spiced, as for the gyros from the Old Olive Tree, that was incomparable—when the fat and earthiness of the meat came together with garlic, oregano, cumin, marjoram, rosemary, and thyme, then it was plopped atop tzatziki sauce (the only yogurt I ate, because I didn't know then that it was yogurt) and a fresh, pillowy pita. Yes, there was nothing better than lamb, when I didn't think about the lamb itself.

—

In my early vegetarian experiments, I was taken to a vegan restaurant called Foodswings in Williamsburg by friends, and because I loved lamb so much, I wanted to try their seitan gyro. How bad could wheat gluten made with the same spices, cut the same way, be? It was too uncanny for me to eat beyond one bite, and this—years before I'd make the full transition—let me know that if I were giving up meat, I would be giving it up. There would be no imitation that could satisfy the same urges, and my only real meat urge, the one I couldn't fathom giving up, was lamb.

There is little factory farming involved in the raising and slaughter of sheep. They're raised on grass, as they're supposed to be, unlike cattle, who are often grain-fed in the industrial system that the corn and soy farmers rely upon to keep them in business; it's a cheap way of fattening the cattle. Lamb is neither as cheap nor as common, though the fact that they feed on mother's milk and grass alone means there's less money for a farmer to spend: They're not buying grain. Those who eat it understand its sense of occasion and perhaps even its seasonality, coming as it does around the spring equinox, in time for Easter.

A lamb is usually slaughtered at six to eight months to provide forty-six to forty-nine pounds of meat. They're adorable animals, all covered in white fluff with their telltale white ears. At Easter time, when they're most often eaten as a celebration of spring and Christ's resurrection, they're also depicted alive—in decorations, on cakes, where their fur is buttercream and their faces different pieces of pastel candy. The lamb, slaughtered; the lamb, beloved. Both at the table, for dinner and dessert.

In regions where there isn't sufficient land for cattle to roam, lamb is a popular meat. "It is rare to find anything but lamb at butcher shops in this part of the world; there isn't enough grazing land for cows, and goats are too destructive to keep in large, uncontrolled flocks," wrote Anissa Helou in *Saveur* in 2009, about the prevalence of sheep in North Africa and the Middle East. Sheep were likely first domesticated in the region over 11,000 years ago, for meat, wool, and their milk. She notes that after leaving her native Lebanon, she found lamb to be treated simply in the West or quite rare in the United States outside of restaurants. Perhaps this was because it was, as she writes, an "expressive" meat—a meat that tasted of the ground it once lived upon, a meat that couldn't be boxed in.

Our cultures provide our tastes and preferences, but our cultures are informed, bound to our lands. Why was I so into lamb as an American child? Why didn't I reject its gaminess, its terroir, its evidence of life? It wasn't a preternatural degree of sophistication. It was simply part of my own initial making, at the hands of grandmother, mother: a taste for it was regarded as natural, a birthright.

"Nothing can be as local as what emerges from the terroir of a single self," wrote Charlotte Druckman, when covering the Pauillac lamb of Bordeaux. I read about these lambs from a French region known mainly for wine and realize Charlotte has told me about this piece before, about the notion of a *terroir of the self*. It's the kind of idea I get excited about, that we all reflect the flavors of those places where we lay down roots, the flavors of all our meals and lessons and curiosities. I hadn't realized this came from reporting on lamb; likely she hadn't told me because I don't eat meat, and friends assume I'll be upset that not everyone on earth is a vegetarian yet.

These Bordeaux lambs are born of sheep who graze on the riverbanks; after subsisting solely on mother's milk for two and a half months, they're slaughtered. Without any grazing, they're less gamey than one might expect. Lamb is specific like this. In Iceland, prized flocks of sheep wander the island until September, when they're herded into their specific farms. This is when the lamb, a local commodity so economically prized it has a Designation of Origin from the European Union, is killed. "Icelandic lamb" or "íslenskt lambakjöt" is certified to its terroir, to the local processes. The lamb is not protected from slaughter, but from economic competition and market confusion.

Older breeds of sheep only give birth once per year to one to two lambs. Their birthing season tends to come in the spring, and come summer, the ewes will finish milking, go into heat, and then become pregnant again by a ram. The lambs that become meat are usually the males, who won't be producing more, though one or two will be saved to continue the cycle of birthing. When they're no longer producing lambs, sheep lose their purpose. But lamb—it's desirable for maintaining its terroir on the plate, for giving up its short life.

That's the interesting thing about prized livestock: It's not for their own sake that they're special. But lamb having this status in so many cultures as important, as specific, might be why it's not common in the United States, where industrial agriculture and grain-fed livestock are prioritized for efficiency and profit, not flavor.

—

I want to know why my grandma loved lamb and served it the way other Americans might put beef or ham on the table, but there's no good answer. "She adopted a lot of traditions on her own," my uncle Rich said. Though she grew up in a house among German family, the Hoelzers, there was no one overarching ethnic influence on her cooking. Like I didn't have the typical Puerto Rican abuela, I didn't have a grandma either who passed on some sort of culinary tradition beyond curiosity, dedication, and care. Every time I go looking for my culinary roots, I hit rock at her: We eat this because grandma did; we make it this way because grandma did. My ethnic culinary lineage begins in Brooklyn and ends out in Smithtown, with a tributary leading down to the Caribbean.

She had more she wanted to do in her life than raise children, maybe—more to offer. "This woman gave up her whole life for us losers," my mom said over a martini. What I can imagine is that she used food to travel and to learn from within the confines of the suburban family home. I might have inherited this through genetics, but here, I think, nurture did more of the work to gradually nudge me toward food. To make food the thing that would finally make me a little bit more free, like I'd hoped for.

—

Though lamb had been the last meat that I could give up, I did give it up. That meat, that dead baby animal, that I thought I couldn't live without: I could. I could live without so many things I'd become convinced I needed, that I thought were integral to the person I am. This is what my twenties were about: assertions, refusals, course corrections. I could be single; I could be platinum blond and bare my skin; I could give up lamb and not replace it with seitan.

I'd worried that because I didn't fit the mold of a food writer I saw a magazine like *Lucky Peach* establishing, I couldn't write about food at all. But then I realized that my eager omnivorous upbringing had provided my tongue enough context already: I knew what people were after when they replaced the lamb with seitan; I knew where the failures were, the nuances, the imbalances. My veganism wasn't so animal-rights-driven that I wouldn't eat at an omnivorous restaurant with a great vegan dish, and that also meant I wouldn't pretend a dry cupcake was good when it wasn't. I'd gone vegan because I'd found out I could do so without really sacrificing my obsession with food, with the joy that it provided me every single day. Couldn't I use food writing to show people this was possible?

My first pieces focused on the things I'd learned running a vegan bakery: That profile of Lagusta Yearwood, my icon, and a personal essay about the chocolate chip cookies that launched my microbakery got me going. Soon I was traveling to San Juan on my own, with a reporter's notebook stolen from the supply closet at the magazine and no real knowledge of how to do travel reporting. But I took vacation time and used credit card points earned buying myself a new laptop to go on my first reporting trip in 2015, to write about chef Paxx Caraballo Moll for Vice. They were featured in a documentary called *Mala Mala* about trans life on the archipelago and were also cooking vegetarian food with local ingredients at a spot called El Departamento de la Comida. I put on my best Bourdainian posture and mapped my vegan self onto it. I faked it.

So much of that work I did at first, I'm not proud of: None of it was copyedited or fact-checked or even really edited. I became a cog in the digital media machine, churning out little pieces to keep the content coming out at a brisk pace. A month after that first reporting trip to San Juan, though, I finally quit my copyediting job to move to *Food & Wine*, where I'd also be copyediting but would at least, I thought, learn how a glossy food magazine worked. It wasn't exactly the experience I'd hoped for, as I was strapped to my computer just like at *New York* and was still too shy to know how to network. But I took advantage of one editor who had actually read my work for other outlets and got a byline with some piece called "Why 2016 Is Going to Be the Year of Vegan Cheese." It was a surprise hit, and I left with that knowledge under my belt to go part-time as an editor at *Edible Brooklyn*, a local magazine with a more agricultural bent to its coverage.

What I hoped to do in food writing was normalize vegan food, make it part of regular coverage. When I got an email from an editor with the subject line "Food writing for the Village Voice?" in March of 2016, it was specifically to have me write about vegan restaurants and cocktails in the city. I started out by going up to the Bronx to cover an ital grocer in Eastchester, but branched out to anywhere that served a vegan dish, writing nearly weekly reviews, doing seasonal previews, and writing calendar items. I came in right at the end: The storied alt-weekly was founded in 1955, and print would shut down in 2017, with digital to follow the next year. My name would be on the masthead under "contributing writers" of the last official issue you could pick up for free out of a red box all over the city. In 2021, a billionaire would relaunch it, but it couldn't retain that magic. The fact that I got to experience any of its magic, that I got to spend a year able to expense my review eating, gave me the energy to keep going as a writer and helped me build so much new knowledge around how vegan cuisine was shaping up. I had to pick up a job at a wine bar to make rent once I no longer had their checks to rely on, but I wasn't copyediting anymore: I was out reporting. I was a freelancer, a free agent. I've made "free" do quite a lot of heavy lifting: Few are "free" under a capitalist system, under any system, but at least I could run around the city on assignment with thirty dollars in my checking account and feel a little bit like I was. Manic hubris, indeed. I was finally alive to who I wanted be.

On Oysters

WHEN HE DIED, MY BROTHER BECAME "MY BROTHER." I stopped referring to him by his name. Brian was alive; Brian made jokes. Brian taunted me endlessly, to the point that you might have thought he was older and I younger. Rather, the five years between us both were and weren't a chasm. We spent so much time together over those summers when I'd been in charge of boiling the frozen cheese ravioli or microwaving the hot dogs into shriveled oblivion that I foisted upon him much of my own taste, and there were some things we came to like together. Music videos for Radiohead. Movies like the Whoopi Goldberg and Ted Danson one, *Made in America*, and *Tommy Boy* that were on TV in a seemingly endless loop. We had a shared cultural language; we were a culture of two, communicating about our parents' fights through our eyes across the table and talking in movie quotes. Without him here, he is absence, void. The whole concept of "my brother" is defined by this loss for me.

Brian, alive, is someone I knew and keep sacred. Brian, alive, I can feel the weight of your head on my shoulder. I can hear you say, "I'm Benny Blanco from the Bronx" for no apparent reason as you walk through the living room while I read on the couch. I can see you seated on the edge of my bed, in this apartment you've never visited, because I can conjure you from my great unending love. I cannot will you, though, to tell me how the lamb I made for Mommy's birthday when I was sixteen tasted. This isn't a movie, where ghosts can speak.

Alive, Brian, he hated fish—hated the smell of it from birth. Our palates weren't so different, though our experiences were. My grandma didn't see him turn a year old. We went to a seafood restaurant called Popei's Clam Bar, and he'd cry from the smell, hysterically, mouth agape screaming as if in physical pain; he'd have to be taken outside. My parents began taking us for sushi weekly in the mid-nineties when it became cool in the suburbs and he'd always order the chicken teriyaki while I got the shrimp tempura. His Chinese food order was the similarly bland chicken and broccoli. We related at the Old Olive Tree and Taco Bell, where we both ordered "just meat" on pita-wrapped gyros and hard-shell tacos.

Hating seafood on an island known for its mollusks is an alienating position: You're not going to find many people who can relate to feeling disgust when summer arrives, finally, and you're eating out on the dock of Harbor Crab. There's a freedom, an animal joy in eating the oysters, the clams, the mussels while hovering above the salt water, boats passing, the sun shining. *This is living. This is what we wait all year for.* Ice melting. Beers swigged from bottles. Why weren't you like us? Why couldn't you enjoy it? Am I talking about seafood or am I talking about being alive?

Patchogue, this town we grew up in, made its name on oysters before it made its name in beer. "The oyster industry employed 350 people in 1850 and reached its peak in the production and shipping of oysters in 1895," says the public-library-published *Patchogue: A Brief History*. "Famous Blue Point oysters were canned and shipped from Patchogue all over the world."

Famous Blue Point oysters, a staple on menus since the early 1800s and apparently a favorite of Queen Victoria—they're a "bottom-planted" oyster, meaning they are culled from managed wild beds of shallow water. Their name comes from their original home in the Great South Bay, between Patchogue and Blue Point. They're more commonly found now in the Long Island Sound closer to Connecticut, related to Patchogue only in their name.

—

When I look for information on the history of my hometown, I have to work around the news of a 2008 murder that took place about a mile away from the house I grew up in and still lived in at the time. I'd been celebrating my twenty-third birthday that night at a Mexican restaurant in Huntington with friends, including the brother of one of the eight kids who attacked and stabbed Marcelo Lucero, an Ecuadorian immigrant. Left to bleed to death in the street, Lucero was pronounced dead an hour and a half later, the official cause listed as a four-inch-deep stab wound to the chest. "A Killing in a Town Where Latinos Sense Hate," read a *New York Times* headline five days after Lucero's murder. The one with the knife had played football with my brother. We were close geographically and emotionally.

In this way, the process of researching Patchogue mimics the feeling of being from Patchogue. There's trying to figure out what the town is about other than this murder, a hate crime committed by children enabled by a deeply entrenched anti-immigrant perspective despite the roads themselves having been built by working-class Irish and Italian immigrants in its heyday. Any story not about the murder tends to tell the stories of early 2000s attempts to revive its sleepy downtown, the sleepy downtown that defined my childhood of longing to get the hell out and into the city. During the years since the murder, the village has become unrecognizable: bustling bars and restaurants that are packed on weekends. There is no monument to what happened, no recognition or conciliation—no accountability for what the town's children did to a man who was simply walking with a friend. They papered over a hate crime with upscale burgers, good coffee, and a restoration of oyster culture.

But when I research Patchogue, I also smile to remember the massive, gaudy French restaurant Louis XVI that I begged, unsuccessfully, to be taken to ("no one likes French food," my parents would say, and I knew that couldn't be true) that's now a much more suitable outpost of Mamma Lombardi's for catering weddings. I've found out that the reason this town had and has such a great public library that opened in 1883 was that it had been somewhere once, when oysters and clams were being harvested, when the lace mill was up and running, when the Long Island Rail Road didn't go any farther, so folks from the city came out to go to its bay beach. To try to understand it in a new way has become a process of confronting shame and nostalgia, of regretting a loss I had no part in.

Patchogue was no longer somewhere when my brother and I were growing up, and it wouldn't become anywhere again until after he was gone. During our nineties childhood, it hadn't been somewhere for a while. This was why every time a restaurant or bakery opened up, I wanted to go, I begged to go. I first had chocolate ganache poured over a rich chocolate cake at a bakery whose name I can't recall; it wasn't long-lived. When it didn't have good chocolate cake or a booming oyster business, Patchogue was a place one wanted, desperately, to leave. There was no reason to stay. The sound of the train and the ferry were the constant background score, reminding you that you were stationary. Stuck.

—

I left at that first opportunity, or I left at the first comfortable opportunity as anxious eldest daughter. My brother, aside from his stint at the military school in South Carolina, never did—or not willingly, ever. He spent time in jail in his twenties.

He went into a rehab facility that he repeatedly escaped from. "Brian Kennedy, of Patchogue, was arrested in Patchogue for criminal possession of marijuana in the fifth degree and criminal possession of controlled substance in the seventh degree on Nov. 17," goes the arrest blotter of the Patchogue Patch blog on November 20, 2010. I wasn't living at home then, and my parents' divorce was still a disaster. No one really wanted to tell me what was going on, if they could help it, because it was never good news. I knew my brother smoked weed, I guess—why wouldn't he? I knew my abstinence, a fear of being like my aunt and uncle whose calls came from inside a correctional facility, was the strange behavior. I'd found him once face down on the floor of the den, passed out from pouring booze into Snapple until he was obliterated. I think about it all the time: Was it a preview? A warning I should've heeded? But my twenties—no, they weren't defined by a good time. They were defined by emotional chaos I sublimated through focusing on only what I could control—cookie dough and style guides—and I certainly couldn't control Brian.

As kids, while I was being the good girl, he'd apparently been sneaking out of the house repeatedly, even stealing my parents' cars for joy rides before he had a license. There were times I was aware of his behavior, like when I was tasked with knocking on his friends' doors to find him or my own brick-size Nokia cell phone was ringing off the hook with my mother desperate to know whether I'd heard from him, only to have him show up at a diner like nothing was happening. His friends at the next table would yell "BK!" and I'd be fuming. But most of the time, I was oblivious, lost in my own world. I just knew that my parents were more lenient with him as he got older when the opposite was true for me, and I was both jealous and resentful. It made escape more necessary.

The envy was a twisted thing. Did it make sense to be envious he could step outside societal norms, that he would defy expectation, if it meant that he was in and out of trouble? This relates to the big things—drug use, selling drugs—and also just emerging from his room on the day of our sister's communion with his new girlfriend who'd accidentally spent the night. It's that he would fly into a rage and threaten to kill himself, my mother and I hysterical, holding him back from the closet that held the guns. *You're allowed to explode in front of everyone? You don't need to keep the pain secret?* It's also that he died young. That really pissed me off for the obvious reason that I want him here, alive, and the other reason that I would never have the balls to do the same. People think I'm some rapscallion for writing what I really think: It's probably because I've never felt free to live in any surprising way, to make mistakes. Here is where I'm the freest I can be; you have it in your hands. The blank page: a solution to the messiness of other people. I beat myself up for making mediocre noodles on a random Wednesday. Imagine how I'd curse myself for dying young, leaving everyone so sad, taking the memories with me like he did. A thief.

—

The evidence of my brother's life on the internet amounts to that crime blotter entry and a rundown of his baseball stats as a 2007 college prospect. He was five feet nine inches and 165 pounds—he had a lean frame; this has been committed to the record. "Alicia, why am I such an amazing specimen," he asked me one day with a stupid smirk on his face, trying to piss me off, "and you're..."

"He is a switch hitter with an open stance from the right side. Kennedy uses a small stride and a knee lift trigger to hit," goes the description of his playing. "He has a line drive swing plane and makes consistent contact. Brian has a slightly open stance from the left side with a line drive swing plane. He uses the whole field and had several hits in game action. Kennedy looks to be a better hitter from the right side right now. He has soft hands in the infield with solid footwork defensively. Brian has an accurate arm with a solid release at 80 mph. He needs to attack the ball more and move through on his release." He was rated a 7 out of 8. He was good and he deserved more, but in the picture of him from this day of playing for scouts, his green eyes look so unhappy. He looks a bit, to be honest, insane. He looks like he's in pain.

He was expected to be an athlete. So was I, though to what end it was never clear, but in one of my few protests of my father, I eased out of softball and into pit orchestra to be with my more like-minded peers. On our school breaks when he wasn't working, our father would take us to a field to make us practice, and he wouldn't let us leave until we each fielded ten "perfect" ground balls. I only wanted to hit; I was a powerful hitter. My brother could switch hit, but I could hit home runs. I had that on him. Only now do I think about it as one of my few proper outlets for rage that didn't hurt anyone. Indeed, that was rewarded.

My brother, the athlete. My brother, who did whatever he wanted to do except leave Patchogue. The last two years of his life, I had the desperate feeling that I could bring him back from whatever brink he was on, figure out a way to make him okay enough to not need Xanax or codeine or, eventually, opiates to survive. I'd randomly get phone calls from him where he'd tell me he wanted to write, that he wanted to chronicle his time in jail and rehab. I encouraged him, but on the inside, I was nervous: Wouldn't he be more immediately successful than me because his life was more interesting? Because he was better looking than me? When he gave our mom Chanel No. 5 for Christmas the same year I'd gotten her some fragrance from Comme des Garçons, I fumed: The prodigal son's gifts would always be better than the dependable daughter's. On those calls, though, he'd say, "I have to move to the city," knowing like I did that it was the only way to survive, to put distance between ourselves and the often stifling atmosphere of our family home. Both of us were always champing at the bit for more—more anything—than Patchogue could give. The only difference is that I did it.

—

He needed more thrills than me, that was obvious. Once I'd left Long Island for Brooklyn and was no longer as afraid of drinking, afraid of the genetic propensity toward addiction and alcoholism that I'd long observed, I invited him to come out on a Wednesday at midnight to a bar on the Lower East Side where someone I was seeing was DJing. If there was anyone I knew who would come out on a Wednesday at midnight it was him, and he said he was coming, but he ignored my texts, my calls. I was so angry, so afraid of what it meant that I kept taking free shots of whiskey and blacked out, throwing up all over myself once I'd made it home. It was March 2016.

This would be the pattern until October 18, 2016: I would say, *Come hang out with me.* He wouldn't. He'd go silent. And then, that Tuesday morning, after a few weeks when I hadn't come out to Long Island to see my family because I'd broken my foot, the phone call from our dad: "I have some very, very bad news," he said, and I didn't flinch, thinking my grandmother had died. Her dementia was deep and total; the only word she would say anymore was "mentirosa"—liar. "Brian died."

I stood up and screamed, I was told. I don't remember. I demanded to talk to my mother, who couldn't speak. "Why isn't it Mama?" I asked, referring to my dad's mother. "Why wouldn't it be her? Why isn't she dead?" I was hysterical, irrational, but trying to make reason out of it: Surely there was just a mistake. The wrong person was dead, that was obvious, and we just had to rearrange the situation. I didn't cry immediately; I just shook. I shook as I put together a bag and called Doug to drive me home to Patchogue. I texted friends to tell them, figuring that one of them would tell me it wasn't so; I texted my ex, for some reason, and got mad at his response for being *so him*. So distant. As we drove down the Ocean Parkway, taking the scenic route and listening to Jeff Buckley's *Grace*, a grasping attempt to calm me, I started to get texts from people offering condolences. I didn't know what they were saying because I didn't believe it was real. I knew when I got home it would all be sorted out.

There was nothing to sort out. He was dead—my brother. Brian, gone. Kerry arrived and we all got Taco Bell, though I hadn't eaten fast food in years. My sister and I were tasked with arrangements at the church, where a lady I recognized from childhood asked us to choose songs. I chose the prayer of Saint Francis of Assisi to be sung twice. "Are you sure?" *I don't fucking care*, I wanted to say. *What difference does it make?* I chose "Here I Am, Lord" because Brian and I would groan whenever my mom told us to have them sing it at her funeral. We went to Marshalls for the shirt he'd be buried in, and my mother cried. "It will be the last time she buys him anything," my aunt Diane explained. My mother didn't stop crying and couldn't eat; I'd hold her body that felt increasingly like just bones until she would fall asleep. We went to pick out flowers, and my aunt joked, coping with the tedium of planning a burial, that when she died we should put her remains in a Ball jar.

I survived on shots of Jameson and kept working over

email, filing edits and figuring out what my next vegan restaurant review would be for the *Village Voice*. I was a freelancer and didn't know how to explain what was happening, didn't want to explain or take away the one thing in my life that was still normal. I had quit a part-time gig copyediting for MTV.com by typing into Slack that Tuesday, in shock, "I have to go. Someone died." His wake was at the funeral home at the corner by the first house we lived in, the small white one with the big yard. We'd walked by it once and agreed we'd prefer to be cremated; as I brought in his shoes, the shoes he'd wear wherever he was going, I knew I wasn't keeping his wish. They were so heavy in my hands. He'd be in boots. We'd longed to be dust.

The only good, clear picture of him for his Mass card was from when he was sixteen, a decade prior. I told the funeral director, "Don't shave his beard. It's just that this is the last good picture..." trailing off and breaking down, a constant behavior of the week between his death and his funeral. The fissure, the friction of having to make arrangements for something I still didn't believe was happening. I was responding the way I had when I was five years old and my grandma died: *This is strange and I know you all think something bad happened, but soon we'll find out this was just a ruse.* I would swallow up the sadness again, swallow up enough of it for all of us to keep living.

When it was time for the wake and I saw his body, I started to scream again. Or so I'm told. Everyone else somehow knew to cry, and I was still in some kind of denial. I didn't want to look at his body; I didn't want to believe it. Even in this moment, why couldn't I just act like everyone else? I wasn't mourning this dead body. I guess this is when he became the void: *my brother*. Brian, something else. This didn't stop me from putting every bracelet on my wrists into the casket with him, an urge I couldn't fight, an urge that felt so primal. *Take these*, I thought. *You need them more than me.* He's buried less than a mile from the house we grew up in, the chaos he wanted to escape. If I'd had my wits, if I'd had any money, if I'd been able to get through to my parents in that time, I always think, I would have insisted he finally be free of this place. That he be cremated, as he had told me he wanted when we were teenagers, and then I could've taken him away. I feel nothing at his gravestone and so I never visit—why, when I can conjure Brian, should I visit the grave of my brother?

—

In the weeks after his death, I started to have panic attacks. The first one came on out of nowhere. My breath was suddenly shallow, my heart was racing, and I wondered aloud: *Will I die without ever eating a mozzarella stick again?* Brian always wanted me to give up being vegan, always offered me a bite of his chicken. We'd come together as kids on those orders of "just meat" tacos and gyros. Before he passed, I'd already been faltering on why I was eating cashew cheese when cows were local or refusing happy chickens' farm-raised eggs. Now, in the nihilism of my grief, I raged at my self-denial. Why should I die without eating a mozzarella stick again? Why should I order the slice at Paulie Gee's with the vegan mozzarella that didn't have any satisfying pull, that just lay on the sauce, limp, barely melting and never browning? What had being good ever gotten me, eh?

It wouldn't be the mozzarella that first got me to go vegetarian after years of strict veganism: It would be the oysters, symbol of Patchogue and home. The famous barman Sasha Petraske of Milk & Honey had passed away unexpectedly, and his wife, Georgette Moger-Petraske, finished his book, *Regarding Cocktails*. There was a party somewhere near the Flatiron just a couple of weeks after my brother's funeral, and I decided I should try to get back into something resembling life. I wasn't dressed for the occasion—a T-shirt, wide-legged American Apparel pants that were basically sweats, and my fake leather H&M jacket had red paint on it from a time I leaned on a pole at the LIRR Jamaica station, not noticing the WET PAINT sign right in front of me. I had decided to go with it. I ordered a Manhattan, as I was in a time of trying all the classic cocktails I'd never gotten around to, and I went to sit by the window by myself. (My social anxiety had gotten better, but I still couldn't, and can't, mingle.)

To pair with the classic cocktails, there was a huge table covered in ice and oysters, shuckers set up behind it in white coats and paper hats. I remembered our childhood; I remembered Brian's screams at the smell of seafood and my delight at summer meals on the bay, my love for those fried clam strips. It couldn't have been my first oyster, but it might as well have been: I couldn't really remember how to eat one. I wanted one, though, desperately. I wanted to taste sea, taste life. I was so angry at Brian for what he'd done, for his unanswered texts and not getting his shit together to leave Patchogue and for getting into opiates, for God's sake, when we knew what those did to people, when our own aunt and uncle had fallen prey to this very thing. He always offered me a bite of his chicken; to spite him, I left veganism behind for an oyster instead. My head tilted back, I slid the meat down my throat. Like riding a bike. Immediately, I left the restaurant. I didn't know who I was anymore, but I liked it.

In Hinduism and Buddhism, mourning may be marked by a period of abstinence from meat. During Lent, in Catholicism, we're supposed to stop eating meat on Fridays to acknowledge Christ's sacrifice. This gives us great pizzas, topped with fried calamari or lemony clams, as seafood is allowed. Maybe that urge for an oyster, and all the urges after it, were a way of reclaiming my appetite from the immense sadness. A way of saying, "I'll live, and I'll live enough for both of us, but because I'm mad at you, I'm going to eat the food you hated most."

Oysters became a secret obsession, the focal point of my mourning keeping me alive, as I was worried that anyone finding out that I wasn't a *real* vegan anymore would hurt my nascent writing career and squash my emergent beat as a vegan who really knew something about food and cooking. A restaurant in my Crown Heights neighborhood, Mayfield, did happy hours, and I became a regular fixture. An oyster bar opened in Patchogue, the old industry back and bustling again, and I would take the train out for lunches with my mom and sister before anyone crowded inside.

Writing about oysters, though, is something of a food writer rite of passage: M.F.K. Fisher did it; Anthony Bourdain did it. Finally, in these oysters, I had forebears to read who could explain this fascination to me; I thrilled at the opportunity to indulge a cliché rather than make a case for trying a dish made with fresh tempeh. Even if I'd intended to keep it secret, I was quietly, secretly, eagerly writing about the oysters bringing me back to life in the wake of death. It had been so stark, the way the oysters gave me meaning again, gave me a focus and something to think about. I had to find all the oyster happy hours; I had to go to all the old oyster bars I'd never even thought about. It became my hobby. I always ordered half Blue Points and half something else, something new to me. I hated West Coast oysters, or so I thought, for being too big—one can't make these kinds of generalizations, but I made them in the beginning, learning how to express myself through my oyster taste as I once had done with apples. I sat at the Grand Central Oyster Bar with the gruff old shuckers; I checked off my selections with pencil on the menus at Maison Premiere. I went to the Mermaid Inn, every location. It was a new vantage point on the city; it was a new language to learn. And I always had my claim to the Blue Points, oyster of my hometown.

During my initial secret forays into the oyster bars of New York City and Long Island, while I was writing a sparse essay on grief and oysters that I actually felt I needed to write, versus all the assignments I took on for money, I researched whether a vegan could eat oysters. The jury was out: These bivalve mollusks didn't have a central nervous system and they were integral in marine ecosystems for cleaning; harvesting oysters and restoring the beds meant better conditions for other creatures. They were local, with a minimal footprint, and, like me, were grounded deeply in New York and its surrounding region, where they were important to the food economy. The logic of veganism for someone ecologically and cuisine minded had been faltering, and oysters were the final sign that I would have to shed another skin, one that had given me so much, that had let me grow.

—

I think of Brian when I eat oysters; they still bring me to him, despite his distaste for seafood. This felt like a dig I could still get in on him, a joke we could still have together as friends, as siblings. But the oyster essay that I was writing in mourning, in secret, was published eventually, and I read it aloud on an NPR food show. This was confusing: Attention and success I had been seeking were now coming through the experience of the biggest loss I ever hope to endure. If I could think of it as little gifts from my brother, a way in which he took part in the slurping with me—a way in which we were still in conversation—then I was able to make sense of it.

Oysters were also helping me repair my relationship to being from Long Island, from Patchogue: They gave me something good to hold on to, something beyond the dysfunction of family, a dead brother, a cultural desert, a town defined by a heinous murder committed by its own children. They're something good, something alive, to reach toward and define myself. I have the outline of a Blue Point's shell tattooed on my right forearm, and it opens up conversations with folks from coasts around the world. They tell me about their oysters; they show me their tattoos. We bond over the good gift our homes provided, not needing to bring up the rest.

On Martinis

If I think of the love necessary to keep a child alive through its early helplessness, I wonder of the neglect that lets a child die—even an adult is a child to its parents. It's easy to place blame on the people around someone who dies by suicide or overdose. The people who are around, who are left behind with their grief and unending love no longer with an object, will be blaming themselves: They will be asking themselves questions without answers until they die. I am the older sister of a dead baby brother. Did I deserve this because I didn't pay close enough attention, because I was staying away to protect myself and the something-like-peace I'd built around my life? I'd get drunk and admit my worry for him. Then, I got drunk in desperate mourning. Now, I drink martinis to have honest conversations with my mom. These aren't subjects to discuss sober.

The stigma of having a dead child is one I see weighing my mom down. *What keeps her going?* thoughtless people asked in the wake of my brother's death. *Two living daughters, maybe*, I'd think, cursing anyone who thought we should also lose our mother, that she should sacrifice herself on a pyre for her sins. So many people wondered about us, gossiped about us for having the ability to continue living through something they couldn't imagine. What did they know about it? But whenever a famous person who's been through the same dies—Sinéad O'Connor, Lisa Marie Presley, Tina Turner—my mom says, "She lost her son." This translates to, *I know their desperation for release from this despair; I know they feel better now.* It's a despair I can't know, a despair I refuse to know: My loss and hers are not the same, though we speak of our grief for the same person.

I may have swallowed my sadness for my grandma as a child, but I decided I couldn't swallow this sadness, this grief. It is too big; it won't fit down my throat. I've shouted through it and maybe always will, refusing any embarrassment or shame and forcing the world to look at what I live with, what so many people live with. I imprinted my grief upon oysters, and I've imprinted it upon martinis made with gin and garnished with olives. It's with these martinis that my mom and I can speak of my brother, of my grandma, of the happy home she tried to make for us and why nothing went according to plan.

—

Gin was the first alcohol I ever tasted. I sat at the kitchen table in my grandpa's house some time after Grandma had passed and picked up a rocks glass that I thought was filled with Sprite. Instead, it was his gin and tonic. I found it disgusting: bitter, tannic, burning. It would've been Beefeater, always Beefeater for my grandpa and now for me, and maybe Schweppes or Canada Dry or Seagram's tonic. This was the early nineties and the cocktail renaissance was still years away; artisanal tonic water made with just a touch of organic cane sugar hadn't yet been ushered into the fold. The sweet syrupyness of the tonic combined with the dry bitterness from quinine—it was like nothing I'd ever tasted. I didn't say anything to anyone, worried as always about having done something potentially bad, and went on to find some actual soda.

Despite a youth of teetotaling, I'd come to quite enjoy drinking in my Brooklyn years. I liked beer, but it always felt so heavy, and so I ripped off my friend Nick's whiskey soda order and made it mine. Once I was writing about food, I started to be assigned cocktail pieces, too: On my first reporting trip to San Juan, in 2015, Vice asked me to write about the piña colada and told me I could expense one so long as it only cost seven dollars. I had to drink a few, but I stumbled into a bar that I was told would be good—a bartender there had set a drink on fire once for a friend. It was called La Factoría, and I immediately loved it for its lack of air-conditioning, its dilapidated walls, the lights strung above the bar midway up to the high-beamed ceiling. Someone named Mario made me a cocktail with beet juice called Beauty and the Beet: "Do you like mezcal?" he asked me, and I lied: "Yes."

It turned out I did like mezcal—the smoke of the spirit met its equal in the earthy sweetness of beet—and I liked the feeling that continued through the night as I was made a "hip" unfrozen take on the piña colada, which originally isn't blended anyway, and served many more drinks as the bar filled up through the night. In what seems like some sort of prophecy, I was introduced to a cocktail historian that night, but I didn't know anything, so I had nothing to say to him. I was also drunk. When I realized I still had one classic piña colada to drink before the trip was over, I left for the Caribe Hilton to drink it. A retired firefighter on vacation offered to pay for it, and considering how cheap Vice was, I let him before running off again to the taxi: I'd convinced the driver to wait for me with my drunk Spanish. He laughed at me and with me.

Studying cocktails and spirits involves a lot of on-the-ground research, and I got back to New York City with a mental list of places to check off. Once my rushed and absurd piña colada piece was out, publicists started to email me and invite me to more cocktail bars, to spirit tastings. I eagerly went, wanting to know more, and finding myself increasingly enamored of a business that was often a man's job: writing about drinks.

What I had found on this assignment was that I liked being in cocktail bars, so I set about studying up. Veganism and baking had opened me up, giving me a way to interact with both my immediate surroundings and the political intricacies of global agriculture; writing about cocktails let me start to travel. After Brian passed, I took the energy from this first reporting trip and continued to ride it by going on a trip every single month, sometimes paid for by me and oftentimes by an alcohol brand. On a tour of Scotland funded by a whisky brand, I learned how to shuck oysters: I was quick and clean at the work.

My palate was good at tasting cocktails. While I'd struggled, always, with really caring about wine beyond having a glass to wind down from a stressful day, cocktails and spirits I came to with ease. I could discern differences between rums of Jamaica and Puerto Rico, between whiskey of Ireland and whisky of Scotland, between the mezcal styles of various agaves and all the intricacies therein. I thrilled to learn about how these were not just products of colonialism or a vast corporate conspiracy to keep people wasted, but as significant to culture and well-being as food. I learned to ask, at distilleries, about evaporation rates, or what's called the angel's share—the amount lost to the air as a distillate ages in barrels: They'd be low in the Scottish climate, which allowed for longer aging and more gravitas for the whisky, and higher in the humid Caribbean, keeping rum with a reputation for being pirate's swill.

—

At first, given the way my cocktail writing began with the piña colada, I had an allegiance to rum for its underdog status. Pirates, the tropics—these were signifiers I liked and wanted to be associated with—but it also came with a mixing problem, basically that I didn't want to drink Coca-Cola. (It's also true that in my early Brooklyn days, a rum and Coke was for some reason my go-to before I made questionable choices fueled by spirit and corn syrup.) Whiskey came second, because I have this Irish last name and it goes so well with club soda; it's an easy drink to quaff when out for hours dancing.

But now the spirits world had opened up to me: I liked mezcal, could handle some tequila, and eventually got put on to gin—the gin I'd long associated with my grandpa—by Negronis. Once I was into gin, there was no turning back. Its dry juniper and herbaceousness made it feel good on the palate, like food, something substantial. The cocktails that were made with it, too, always made me feel like I actually knew what I was doing. Variations and twists and mixology of the sort that sees things being set on fire had gotten boring after a while, and I wanted the classics. I was drinking all of them: Negronis, gimlets, and eventually martinis. Real martinis, made with gin and dry vermouth. At first, I changed my orders up here and there. I had a tactic where at a new bar, I'd order something off the menu to see about their creativity and then order a gin martini to see how they could do a classic. But soon enough I would only ever order a gin martini. It is all I want, in all seasons, in all cities. The photo archive I keep in the cloud shows them in various states of blur in Edinburgh, Mexico City, Rome, and beyond.

Martinis appealed for their sense of occasion and gentle absurdity—those ridiculous pointed glasses! At more serious bars, they were in a breast-shaped coupe or a bell-like Nick and Nora, exuding elegance. I liked being a bleached-blonde, curly-haired, tattooed young woman from Long Island and ordering a cocktail once associated with the upper crust. They told me about how serious the bartender was by the questions they did or didn't ask; they told me what the bartender thought of me and my drinks' know-how by the questions they did or didn't ask, by whether they listened to me when I said "gin" or assumed vodka because of my gender and served me something utterly undrinkable. I never want to assume a bartender will shake a martini just because of James Bond's famous Vesper order, but at this point, I have to make sure to ask for it stirred, because I can't stand an overdiluted, icy martini. It's a simple drink of three ingredients—gin, dry vermouth, ice—that tells a grand story, every time it's made.

—

Recipes for the drink began appearing in cocktail manuals in the 1880s, and it quickly assumed its stature as *the* cocktail to rule them all despite coming late to the scene, after Manhattans, mint juleps, sherry cobblers. At first, all vermouth had color, but eventually it would be filtered out, and the martini as we know it—clear—would come to be, and it would long maintain its status as the choice of what had been known as a "Clubman," a society person of good breeding. The mid-twentieth century would see a dwindling interest in the cocktail as it came to represent a stuffy Americana from an older generation, and all their values were under scrutiny by younger folk interested in the counterculture. In the eighties and nineties, martinis would be more closely associated with vodka and all sorts of flavored variations—the espresso martini, notably. The early 2000s would see the London-born Porn Star martini come into vogue, made yellow with passion fruit liqueur and served with a sidecar of Champagne. These would all dilute the cultural understanding of what a martini is: All of a sudden, it was made with vodka and on menus with various fruit flavors. To be a martini meant to be served in a martini glass, and nothing more. Conditions have improved, but I know when I walk into a place whether it's going to be a martini or a whiskey soda that I order, falling back on my old standby to ensure I'm not the asshole asking for a fancy drink in a dive, though sometimes I do want to go totally retro and order a lychee martini when it's on offer.

For reasons that are likely obvious, studying the history of cocktails and spirits is difficult business because you need to have had someone sober enough around to write things down. That results in various stories for any subject, and gin is no exception. Does it go back to the Middle Ages, or just seventeenth-century Holland? Was it a medicinal liquor, safe to drink when waterborne disease ravaged England? Likely, it was all of these things, but the gin we think about as the gin of a martini is a London dry gin—as my grandfather put in his gin and tonic. It's decreed by law that to be called "gin," the dominant note must be juniper and it must be bottled at no less than 40 percent alcohol, but all gin-makers have their secret lists of botanicals that provide the less pungent notes. Beefeater, being so juniper-forward, is my favorite. Perhaps genetic, perhaps nostalgic. My grandpa started drinking martinis in the seventies. "After dinner, I used to make a martini," he says, with no further explanation for his own tastes.

—

A martini tends toward the unknown, just like its chief component. Robert Simonson, in his book *The Martini Cocktail*, writes, "The two central facts about the Martini are: it's the most famous cocktail in history, and we don't know where it came from." I love that about it, its commitment to both being obscure and signifying so much. The martini provides conversational fodder and argument about ratios, garnishes, ingredients, history in a way that no other cocktail does—it is such a stoic drink, in the end, standing up to all the commotion. What never changes about it is its significance to the drinkers of the world, who all have an opinion on the right way to serve one. (Mine is a two-to-one ration of Beefeater gin to Dolin dry vermouth, stirred until icy cold, with an olive garnish but not dirty—not dirty is key.) The martini becomes something different in every bartender's hands, because even the most studied martini-maker will have a different gauge for when it's just the right temperature than the next; it becomes a new drink every time, over hundreds and thousands of cocktails served, because we're different whenever it comes to meet our lips. Yet we can rely on it.

One of my great-grandmother's maiden names was Serviss, which is Scottish, apparently, but of perhaps French origin, deriving from a nickname given to a brewer or barkeeper. When I learned this, I felt an alignment within myself—the kind of alignment between who I am and where I come from that I'm always seeking out. My culinary lineage might be fragmented, and no one has any deep reasons for why they like things, but I want to believe there's a brewer or barman or barmaid in there. An ancestor cheering on my found vice, which, when finally found, I made into a point of work and research. But could that account for how aligned I felt when finally stepping into a cocktail bar on assignment? Or do I just like to drink? There are mysteries, like how a spirit came to be, that are richer stories when they're left unknown.

—

Alcohol in most cases is one of the most wasteful things one can consume, producing twelve times the wastewater for the amount of spirit created. It goes against the grain of all my concerns for me to drink so much of it, and to drink a standardly produced one such as Beefeater. I justify it as I do my use of plastic pens: I make deeply considered choices around consumption in most areas of my life. When I travel, I try to drink the small-batch gins if they're on offer. There are some things I just won't compromise on.

There have been studies suggesting we should drink gin distilled from peas, which could reduce carbon dioxide emissions. Gin could be made from whatever can be distilled wherever one is. That is one mark in favor of it, versus other alcohol: Whereas rum is made from sugarcane juice or molasses, depending on the style, and whiskeys are grain-based, gin can be made from any base ingredient. The chief characteristic of gin is its juniper flavor, a tree that's native to the United Kingdom and grows in dry, rocky areas. Many new, boutique gins have also taken to using local botanicals for their flavorings, cutting back on the dependence on imported ingredients. It's an adaptable spirit, giving hope for a future full of martinis.

—

Coming to gin, to martinis, after I returned to eating oysters and bivalves, seemed to make sense. Martinis and oysters are a classic pairing: Both feel so New York, and briny oysters complement the dryness of a good, cold martini. There are few places where you're going to find oysters that don't serve martinis, too, and good ones where they know what they're doing—where they ask the right questions of the guest. They feel like home, or a homecoming.

My mom, sister, and I began to have a routine once I started to eat oysters again: I'd take the Long Island Railroad from Nostrand Avenue in Brooklyn to Ronkonkoma or Patchogue on a Saturday morning, they would pick me up, and we'd go straight to Catch by eleven-thirty a.m., an oyster bar that opened up in town just in time for me to make my prodigal return to oysters. We'd make our orders of oysters, po'boys, martinis—or a soda for my sister, before she turned twenty-one—and wonder aloud about what had happened. We'd make space to miss Brian openly, in a space that allowed us our grief no matter how much time passed, and we'd talk about him as though he were alive, reminiscing about locking ourselves in the bathroom when he pretended to have a dead mouse in his hand that he was chasing us with. (How fun he was when he wasn't expected to be manly and mature!) We'd make a space where it was finally safe for us to have feelings and express them, that thing that had been denied us for so long, until a loss so big it showed us the mistake we'd been making all along. A generational mistake, perhaps a genetic mistake, but one that couldn't be repeated if we were going to keep living. And though I know my mom sometimes thinks she'd rather not have lived through losing my brother, I want her to stay with us as long as she can, even when I'm so mad at her I can barely see straight. I can be mad at her because she's made it okay to be.

There's really no reason to be mad. When I feel haunted by all that wasn't done for Brian to ensure that he would still be here today, I blame her, I blame myself, I blame my dad. But I don't know what to do with this blame. And I need a martini just to acknowledge that it's there.

She has no explanation for the miseries, the way my grandpa doesn't know why he drank martinis in the seventies, the way we don't really know who invented the drink in the first place. When my parents did finally get divorced, it was horribly unamicable and very traumatic for all of us—especially my then-young sister. I have guilt because throughout my upbringing, as touched by fear of my father's anger and irrational demands as it was, some semblance of normalcy was maintained; I was able to go to Catholic school, play the violin, and go on a high school orchestra trip to France that set me up with expectations for my life that took me up and away. My brother, whom I saw as difficult when he was actually troubled, never got the help he needed. My sister, only eight years old when they divorced, feels such a rupture, such a resentment toward both of our parents, for what they put her in the middle of—and then she lost her big brother when she was only sixteen, compounding the pain, and is only putting herself back together in her twenties. But then I think: My young life was more or less uninterrupted until money became scarce when I was in college, and I still needed to put myself back together—to become myself without fear of ridicule, of rage. Is it life? Or is it this family? *All happy families are alike*... I'm the sober one in this history, trying to write it down, but getting any closer to the truth requires a drink. I see why these cocktail stories are so muddled, blurry, diffuse.

My sister, now in her twenties, is really good at feelings. For all my desire to be more open, more honest, I'll never have quite the knack for it that she does—such a knack that it often makes people uncomfortable, and still I'm envious of it the way I was jealous of Brian's ability to stir things up. I've inherited the notion that feelings are embarrassing; feelings are messy; that we should only bring them up in the right contexts. My grandpa doesn't go deep, whether I ask about cocktails or why he married my grandma, why he had children: "It was what you did."

I always took to my diaries to express emotions, as they would be unseemly and despised in regular conversation. Anger, yes: Anger was a fine emotion, for my father. The rest of us worked around that. But anything else needed to be expressed in secret, and music was the method. In Radiohead and Jeff Buckley, I found emotional solace, assurance that I wasn't alone in feeling alone; it was in magazines that I tried to learn about culture beyond my immediate surroundings, which were desolate; it was in a romantic relationship that I could find some way of being immersed in what felt like stability. It was only in eating, in talking about what we were eating, that my family was safe expressing themselves, their likes and dislikes. We could have our preferences when it came to food, and they would be indulged to the point that my mom would send me to school with a salad and fried chicken in my lunchbox because I didn't like sandwiches. My brother could scream at the seafood joint. My sister could, to everyone's amusement, ask for salmon sushi from her high chair the way I once asked for lobster. Opinions about apples were encouraged; everyone's favorite Entenmann's was on the counter. Food continues to be the safe place for expression. Now, we drink, too.

—

There's no way of bringing my brother back from the dead, but it does seem like we try to rewrite the story when we sit down to a dozen Peconic oysters and martinis. I don't see the purpose of holding a grudge against my mom—she has suffered enough. But sometimes a heat, a rage, a desperation burns up in me: *Why didn't you fix it?* It's not fair, though I still want to ask the questions, and we only have the courage under these circumstances. Gin, medicinal again.

Without answers there is just ongoing conversation, an acceptance of how the way we used to deal with things didn't result in anything going the way we wanted. How do we pretend to be a normal family without my brother? We were never a normal family in the first place... *every unhappy family is unhappy in its own way.* Over oysters and martinis, we find a way to talk about it; mostly, though, we revel in our aliveness, our togetherness, as a miracle, as a means of celebrating the survival of the worst thing that happened to us. We try to be a better family than we were for Brian, more honest about the questions even if we don't have the answers.

On Mushrooms

THE FIRST TIME I ADOPTED A BOURDAINIAN POSTURE and went to San Juan on a reporting trip in 2015, that piña colada assignment opened up cocktails to me—and then I was off to the races, traveling anywhere and everywhere that would have me. The travel I'd once dreamed of eventually became a form of running away, of not sitting with grief. These just seemed to be the circumstances of my life: The only things that pushed me forward were also forms of loss. My grandma gave me a love of food but passed by the time I was in kindergarten; my parents' divorce led me toward baking; a breakup ended the bakery; the end of the bakery got me to write about food; and my brother's death inspired an essay that people paid attention to. I am often confused about whether I just make the best of my circumstances or it's sick to never simply take to bed and endure the sadness. How would I emerge from that, from rest? Who would I be? It's a luxury, anyway, that I have never been able to afford.

Most of those trips I was taking were back and forth between San Juan and New York, and I came to intimately know how to most efficiently and cheaply get from JFK to SJU and back again. Perhaps it seemed inevitable that I'd make the move: On every trip, I would gaze longingly into people's tropical apartments, imagining how I'd decorate like an Almodóvar heroine and happily sweat through my workdays. The humidity of Puerto Rico, my paternal grandmother's birthplace, kept my allergies at bay and made my curls coil stunningly without any product. The archipelago called me to it through assignments, as well as the reprieve: In its weather, I breathed freely; staring at palm trees from hotel windows, the weight of mourning lifted from my back. I'd have to understand a new type of death, though, to break this pattern and finally make a choice in my life that wasn't forced by a tragedy. And like any good comedy, it would end with a wedding.

—

The foragers tell me that once I start seeing a mushroom, I will see it everywhere. My first edible mushroom spotting would be a wood ear, known as oreja de ratón in Spanish. Mouse ear. It's growing off a tree in the gardens of Casa Blanca, a home that had been built for Ponce de León in 1521 but where he never actually lived; he died on his search for the Fountain of Youth before he could make it there. His loss is our gain, as its grounds are a cooling, lush reprieve from the San Juan sun. This tree, though, with the wood ears, is right in the line of it, and the round brown mushrooms that cook up to be slick and chewy are scorched.

Another forager once told me that these are perhaps the most common culinary mushroom in Puerto Rico. He kept emphasizing "culinary" on our phone call, and I kept wondering why anyone is concerned with other mushrooms—the ones that kill or sicken—until I remembered that there are also those that heal. The turkey tails, the chaga, the naturally occurring psychedelic compound psilocybin that is produced by more than 200 fungi... My only interest in mushrooms, predictably, is for their culinary potential. At the Grand Army Farmers' Market in Brooklyn, once my local, I would go Saturday mornings and visit the mushroom lady. She had long acrylic nails and offered an array: meaty oyster mushrooms in pink, yellow, gray; frizzled maitake; occasional special items, like hen or lobster of the woods. They were pricey and she was gruff, her tan and New York accent and those nails making her intimidating for the simple fact of the incongruity. Why was this woman in charge of the mushrooms, which seem like such dirty work? I always wanted to pitch a profile of her but never got up the nerve.

On one of my many reporting trips to Puerto Rico, I visited a new business that was cultivating oyster mushrooms called—cleverly—Huerto Rico ("huerto" means, basically, a small garden) for the first time in February 2019. The outfit was located in Bayamón, a municipality not far from the San Juan metro area. I parked outside at the address I had been given, only to find out that this was a residential home.

"I hope I'm not about to get us killed," I half joked to the photographer who was on this assignment with me, when the door opened and Sebastián Sagardia came out in T-shirt, jeans, and baseball cap. He seemed affable, a kindred spirit driven by curiosity rather than stability, and trustworthy. An older woman had allowed him run of this property for free for a few months if he committed to fixing it up, he told us.

The living room was empty, aside from a beach chair, and so I was still nervous. Sebastián opened one bedroom door and it smelled rancid. Bags of white substrate inoculated with cultures to grow the mushrooms hung from the ceiling like punching bags. Though I liked him immediately, I remained trepidatious until the next room opened and it was filled with white air, through which you could see the yellow mushrooms sprouting from the same types of bags we'd just seen. I gasped like a child at Disney World.

Sebastián was cultivating oyster mushrooms after leaving the advertising world, and he was using wood waste and coffee grounds collected from local businesses to do so. The project was tough because the rooms needed to be kept at very specific humidities and temperatures, and Puerto Rico isn't known for stability in either of those (nor for stability in its electrical grid to sustain them artificially, for that matter). There also wasn't and isn't high demand for culinary mushrooms on the archipelago—a massive business called Setas de Puerto Rico cultivates the agaricus varieties, and you can easily find them in huge quantities at Costco or local supermarkets. In the intervening years, Huerto Rico has turned its attention toward a native variety of the reishi mushroom, which is a bit bitter and used more as medicine than food, and could have cancer-fighting properties; that research has garnered them a USDA grant with which they've opened a 4,000-square-foot space in Carolina, in the northeast of the island by the airport. They may also try to cultivate local varieties of oyster mushroom that don't require so much temperature control because they can thrive in the tropical climate. This is all a far cry from the business's start in a Bayamón home.

—

Mushrooms, whether wild or cultivated, bloom from waste like the wood and coffee that gave Huerto Rico its start. This is their beauty and the source of their mystery. They're really the fruiting body of the fungus that is growing beneath the visible surface. When the wood ears are sprouting on that tree, it's because they're emerging from the fungi that is feasting on its decay. It's both beautiful and terrible to consider, and it reminds me of my life's own cycles. But this clear connection, incredible closeness between life and death, might be why there's even a term for "mycophobia," a fear of mushrooms, and so often, culinary varieties are considered distasteful by some. They're fleshy, often chewy, and occasionally really look just like different types of meats. Their uncanniness, their unreadability and mutability—these make them difficult to understand. The people who go down the rabbit hole of mushrooms tend to go deep, and once they do, they start speaking a language that the rest of us have to labor to understand. Good foragers will drive off road randomly because they sense a good spot for chanterelles or truffles. They seemingly become one with the mycelium pulsing underneath our feet. Not classified as vegetables, fungi occupy an interesting in-between space in whether or not they're suitable for vegans, much like oysters: plants that make us reconsider what it means to be alive.

Culinary mushrooms, specifically, are associated with a Eurocentric gastronomic ideal; it makes sense, as the cooler temperatures would allow mushrooms more preservation potential both before being found and after. Psychedelic mushrooms were part of ancient life in Egypt, Greece, and among Indigenous peoples in what's now Mexico. Indigenous tribes in what is now the U.S. and Canada ate many mushrooms: deer mushroom, cooked on hot stones; timber mushroom, fried. Colonialism and Christianization put the kibosh on a lot of the knowledge around fungi because of its psychedelic potential; the privileging of written documentation by clergymen and botanists from Europe suggests much lost information. In Puerto Rico, some of that knowledge is being rebuilt as the local mushrooms are documented, but this rift is a gulf. Haiti is one place in the Caribbean, specifically, where a foraging culture to create the beloved rice dish djon djon persists.

Madeleine Kamman, chef and author of *When French Women Cook*, notes in the 1976 book that "for the last few years," cultivated mushrooms had become widely available, but that wild were always going to be preferable. (The American Mushroom Institute, a trade association for growers of cultivated mushrooms, was founded in 1955.) Many immigrants like herself brought their foraging traditions and knowledge with them, while the "modern" palate of the time was feasting solely on white button mushrooms that had been given the fancy-sounding name champignons de Paris. Kamman recommends numerous resources for the would-be forager, whereas twenty years later, in *The Dean & DeLuca Cookbook*, many of these less prosaic wild mushrooms would come to be commonly cultivated at scale for purchase or there would be folks like the woman at my old Brooklyn farmers' market who'd done the dirty work, offering chanterelle, hen-of-the-woods, morel, and oyster mushrooms. Shiitake had become one of the most widely cultivated in the world. Matsutake (which means "pine mushroom" in Japanese) remains one of the most prized mushrooms: like truffles, it can't be cultivated and must be found in the wild, among conifers, and thus fetches huge sums of money especially in Japan, where it is a prized crop for its "spicy" flavor. By the time Andrea Gentl's *Cooking with Mushrooms* came out in 2022, edible mushrooms were certifiably cool and a growing billion-dollar industry, with kits for growing your own on the countertop becoming wildly popular.

Mushrooms occupy such strange space as a foodstuff: both wild and cultivated, both mundane and special, both expensive and freely given by the earth. Could an apple ever be so rare and significant as to sell for seventy dollars a pound, as

Matsutake did in Kunming, China, in 2022? One ounce of fresh white truffle could cost $249.95—imagine chocolate being that price! Matsutake could become even more scarce owing to drought and high temperatures in the regions where it can be found; hot, dry summers are bad for truffles in France and Italy, too. Scarcity combined with distinct, irreplaceable flavor has made these delicacies. What replaces them—what becomes special to an elite few when they no longer have these to differentiate their plates from everyone else's?

Luxury fungi might become more difficult to find or pricey to access, but mushrooms broadly are part of a vision of the future: Fungi help forests absorb carbon. While agricultural land use is a major driver of climate change owing to loss of biodiversity, the smart use of a combination of forest and edible mushroom cultivation can both create food and capture carbon. Waste from wood-working and coffee-making, as at Huerto Rico, can be reused to sprout oyster mushrooms, and the spent substrate—what's left over in the bags after all the mushrooms have been harvested—can be used as compost. There is a system here that the mycelium networks are already part of, have always been part of: If we tap into them, work with them and with the waste we're already generating, do we have not just a human future on this planet, but a long one?

When I unwrap my portobello mushrooms from Costco, that's what I think about. I also think about how every book tells me these are worthless mushrooms with nothing to offer, while I turn them into so much with nothing but salt, pepper, and oil on my cast-iron. Or I marinate them with the spices of shawarma and put them on the barbecue grill, then serve them with pita and an herb-filled yogurt sauce. Portobellos, because they're common, are *nothing special*. So many have internalized this notion and think they don't really like mushrooms, and I think that's just because they haven't had them prepared properly. I show them that if you treat them like meat, if you put them on a hot pan without adding any fat until they've released their moisture, that they can offer succulent texture and meaty satisfaction without the "proprietary technology" of fantasies about the future of food that include lab meat. But if pretending they're *nothing special* keeps them widely available and affordable, then I'll keep up the charade that they have very little to offer.

I bought a knife once that's intended to be used in mushroom foraging, ever hopeful I might join the foragers' ranks, but it's stuck—it doesn't open, despite removing the safety and watching YouTube videos where I'm assured that it's quite simple. I've handed it to my friend who's handy with knives and asked, "Can you open this?" and he can't. With oysters, I had an inborn knack; with mushrooms, not so much. I inquired of a forager I met in Calgary during a food symposium who carries the same knife about what might be going wrong, and he looked at me with pity. I've given up on foraging, for now, though I want so badly to find some bright orange chanterelles of my own. I tell myself it will open when the fungi gods believe me ready. Clearly, with my eye only good for scorched wood ear, I've not yet been approved. The closest I get to foraging is catching plump, ripe mangoes when they fall from the tree right in front of me. But I keep my eyes open.

While it might seem like common sense to forage if one has the ability, knowledge, and land available to them to do so—and it was indeed common sense for humans everywhere for many years—it had been a fraught activity for legal reasons. Though in the early days of the United States, foraging was so protected that it was legal to obtain food on the private property of others', this wasn't a right meted out equally. Indigenous peoples were the first to be threatened for seeking available food on private property, and after the Civil War, white Southern plantation owners sought to restrict the foraging of newly freed Black citizens in order to force them back to plantation work. Foraging would have provided sustenance as well as the ability to sell what they procured: That wasn't ideal for those who sought cheap labor, and thus eventually there were more and more laws that prohibited foraging under the guise of protecting property rights. In the late 1880s, there were conservation activists who worried that rural white foragers would somehow interfere in nature. Anti-foraging laws in the U.S. have their origin in wealthy folks looking to exploit or control; they're not about protection of the land, and this legal prohibition created a social notion that one who forages is a vagabond or simply strange.

Foraging has come into vogue in recent decades, though, because of an interest in reconnecting to land and because restaurant chefs have seen there is flavor potential and cultural cachet in offering what is wild and uncultivated, in having connections to their own professional mushroom hunters and ramp whisperers in their address books. Social media stars like Alexis Nikole Nelson have taken it upon themselves to educate the public on how to forage, too. What was once outlawed and made odd, now part of our food lives again.

—

When I first visited Huerto Rico, I'd been feeling adrift as the year had begun, and I was starting my days by drawing a card from a tarot deck and journaling my reflections. Regular work, the anchor gigs a freelancer takes on to make sure rent is paid, had been disappearing and drying up. To endure in the meantime, I'd taken a job at a wine bar in the East Village to make up the difference, and was running around taking on any gig I could while putting out a podcast I hoped would help me get my first book deal, to write about the history of veganism in the U.S. The assignment that had me researching mushrooms came about because another website, another contributor writer job, was going under and out with a big bang, paying the columnists with whatever was left over to do a dreamier assignment. (My desire to write about the big three plant proteins—tofu, tempeh, and seitan—in depth hadn't proved as compelling as sending me to Puerto Rico to see whether there was any real hope in the under-resourced agricultural system of the colony.)

Every day, I was feeling restless and pulling these cards,

and getting Death. I knew that it didn't mean that I was in danger, nor anyone close to me—I'd hoped to be spared for a bit, at least—but that some part of my life was coming to an end. I assumed a breakup, or a friendship running its course. While I was on the reporting trip, my grandmother—my father's mom, the one I thought had died when my brother had—passed away, on the same day that I was pointing out a sign toward Mayagüez and telling the photographer, "That's where my grandmother was born."

It wasn't that, though. I kept pulling the card. Death. I waited to see what it might be. Until I knew what it would be, like always, I just worked.

During those months, my sister was attending cosmetology school. She hadn't been ready to go to college (I hadn't been, either), but she had to do something, and so I looked up "best cosmetology school in New York City" and found Arrojo in Tribeca. The founder, Nick Arrojo, was famous for being the hairstylist on *What Not to Wear*. I knew that I wanted Cameron to have a way to get out of Patchogue, so she would stay with me in Brooklyn some days to go to school. Because I was the only person she knew in the city, I became her regular hair model. Under the tutelage of master stylists, she kept me blond and cut my hair into round layers unlike anyone had ever done before. "Make it rounder, make it cooler," her British teacher told her, his hands in my curls like we were in a nineties shampoo commercial. On my couch one morning, I made her give me bangs. It had come to seem self-serving, that I'd made my sister go to hair school, but I looked the best I ever had in my life while also having the least amount of money. That April, she graduated, and I felt, again, like I had some sort of permission—but I wasn't sure to do what. Could I leave New York? Did I want to? I started to consider what a nomadic life could look like.

A few days after her graduation, I went on a trip to San Juan that I hadn't wanted to go on. I simply thought my time of writing about food and drink in Puerto Rico was over, stale, no new stories—or no new stories for me, at least, and I wanted to be focused more on the foundational work that would sell this book I wanted to write. My friend Rafa visited me at the wine bar one Monday night, and I told him I didn't feel good about going, that the trip was about promoting a bar I'd long loved but no longer enjoyed, that I felt strange about how they couldn't hold on to women bartenders and wondered whether there wasn't some toxicity in the workplace. This conversation around hospitality had been bubbling up out of #MeToo, and suddenly I was suspicious of everyone in an industry I'd so eagerly fallen in love with as a writer and a worker.

But I was convinced to go—it's hard to say no to a free trip when you can get someone to cover your shifts, and I had been traveling as much as possible since my brother died. Manic grief, we could call it. It would be me bunking with a cool bartender from Venezuela who was working in Paris, my compatriot on a trip with all dudes who wouldn't look at us much less make conversation. On a trip to the rum distillery Don Q in Ponce, the major city of the south of Puerto Rico,

I wrote in the bus on the way there, sitting in the back and minding my business. While we toured the barrel room, they opened up a cask of some rare aged variety, and I asked one of the local bartenders on the tour to hold up the flask of it so I could take a picture. He posed with it happily, smiling, and not wanting to tell him I needed a picture of the *flask* not of *him*, I took the shot and considered it useless.

This local bartender saw the photo as an opening to talk to me. He'd read the big story about the mushrooms—it had gone out earlier that week. He told me about different pizzas he liked, about his master's thesis on post-colonial international relations, about Jürgen Habermas. He didn't shut up, and then he got on the bus and sat next to me in the back, where he wouldn't shut up some more. There was snot coming out of his nose and he couldn't tell, because he had a thick handlebar mustache, and I saw this, having known this person for ten minutes, and thought, *This will be a funny story when we're together.* I texted Doug and said, "I think this guy is hitting on me..." For me to have noticed, it must have been very obvious. For my mind to have had this random thought about us walking down the aisle because snot was coming out of his nose—I must have just been hungry and tasted too much rum on an empty stomach.

His name was Israel, which I found to be an unfortunate name—biblical in intention and now political in contemporary reality—but after the first night we spent together, he put my shoes on for me while I was wobbly from a hangover. He sat on my suitcase to make sure it closed. I never felt nervous or unsure around him, and for the first time in my life, I could fall asleep with another person touching me. Oh, I hated it! I had thought the death card and Cameron's graduation had meant maybe I was going to be more free—traveling the world, no home, all the possessions put in a garage.

Instead, I made plans to spend just thirty days in Puerto Rico. They turned into sixty, and into a dog named Benny and an apartment. I knew I was done for the time we woke up in my temporary apartment and I asked him, "Are you a person who makes the bed?" and, slightly misunderstanding my existential tone, he threw his Montelobos Mezcal tote bag to the floor and started to make the bed. I'd never been with anyone who didn't make me feel like too much, or too demanding; he'd probably still think I'm too aloof, but whatever. This eager willingness to do what I asked and to take care of me—I didn't know it could exist. I thought life was pulling teeth, white-knuckling through work and grief in the hope of some vague future when it would all make sense. Swallowing sadness like it's an oyster. Drinking martinis to numb the pain. Life is these things, but he made it also seem like there could be something else to it. Something like care, a dreaded word I'd avoided because all it seemed to mean for women was work without pay. With Israel, caring became fun.

I've forced vegetarianism onto him, though he makes some exceptions, mainly for cured meats that have no comparable substitutes. I've tried, with mushrooms, to make something like 'nduja, the spicy Italian pork paste, to no success; I think about aging a mushroom sausage, but where would I do such a thing? Where would I hang my veggie meats? I say, constantly, that I will make mushroom pepperoni for our regular pizza nights, but instead I just take those plain old portobellos and sear them for tacos, for "steak" nights, or brush them in barbecue sauce and put them on the grill as pinchos. I'm still the vegetarian who would rather eat a mushroom being a mushroom, not a meat replacement. As I sometimes say to him when I'm being a bit cheeky and mean: "I gave up New York for you; you can give up prosciutto." The truth, of course, is that this new life I have with him was the fruit of that old life's decay. Our love not a cliché red rose, but a mushroom, the fruiting body of unseen machinations willing us into existence.

On Plantains

I IMAGINED A CARIBBEAN WRITER LIFE AS AN ADULT THE way I imagined a New York City life as a child. I watched *Before Night Falls*, Julian Schnabel's 2000 film about the life of Cuban writer Reinaldo Arenas, over and over. In the film, there is a montage of scenes where Arenas, as played by Javier Bardem, is editing his first novel according to edits from fellow writers José Lezama Lima and Virgilio Piñera. He's pictured on the roof of a Havana apartment eating plain broccoli and boiled eggs, the ocean visible in the background. He's in his room sweating, shirt open, as he reads aloud from what he's written. *This is a writer!* I thought. (I'd thought the same of Rene Ricard as a kid watching Schnabel's *Basquiat*, how he would float into the diner.) In my early twenties, during my brief attempts at writing fiction, I would try to emulate Arenas by way of Bardem's meal as though it would help my writing be any good. I wanted a typewriter. I wanted to feel the roof vanishing as I gave into the *ta-ta incesante* of the keys. I settled for Huntington Village and a PowerBook.

This Caribbean writer life, like a New York City life, felt like something I was owed—something I was due, something I should inherit. Why did everyone who came before me in my family get these exciting places to live, to grow up, and I got Patchogue, the failure of an oyster village? Even my mom who grew up in Smithtown had her childhood summers in Bay Ridge to look back on; my best friend Kerry lived in Astoria, Queens, before she moved out to our miserable town and went back for annual block party stickball games. When I thought about my childhood summers, I thought about the meals of microwaved hot dogs my brother and I ate while I subjected him to another nineties movie about drag queens that was always on TV. I thought about an adolescence trapped in a bedroom with just a boombox and my Delia*s journal when I wasn't working in a windowless room making eight dollars an hour under the table at my mom's job in Hauppauge. The best summer of my life was in 2003, the year of the blackout across the northeast, when we kept constructing ever-longer slip and slides and lived on chicken fingers from the Metropolis Diner on Route 112. During the blackout of 1977, which my Manhattan father lived through, he had to walk home in the dark from a Mets game at Shea Stadium in Queens and arrived to news of the Son of Sam serial killer's emergence onto the streets—to me, this was a life. This was a story to tell, not unlike my grandmother Rosa's tales of a childhood in her aunt's house that shook from the practice of Santería.

By raising me in Patchogue, I was being given a life without stories. As my parents saw it, I was being spared danger. But I would have my lives. My inheritance would never be a large sum of money; at the very least, it could be justification for moving to new cities.

—

I'd always been interested in what it meant to be Puerto Rican but not all the way Puerto Rican. It wasn't uncommon where I grew up to be multiethnic. One of my good friends in elementary school also had a Puerto Rican dad and a white mom. I saw Mariah Carey, fellow Long Islander, on TV be described as "biracial" and thought, *That's what I am.* It was such a relief, to have a word for parents whose skin is different colors, whose hair is different textures. But it just wasn't talked about, ever. My parents had the perspective that these things didn't matter, that they wouldn't influence how we existed in the world, even if that same world was telling us, "Your parents are different."

I put it in a box marked "do not discuss" where it was filed with the fact of my grandma being dead. That's how I became endlessly confused about what was mine to claim and what wasn't. As I got older, and especially when I ended up repeatedly coming to the archipelago as an adult during a time when one's ethnic identity was an essayist's currency, this became more confusing; over time, the lack of clarity has felt more like a secret weapon.

Not knowing who I was or what I could claim, I focused on just enjoying the food. In the food, always, there was freedom to speak and embody. No one could tell me I didn't like something I was eating; no one took food out of my hands. The reality of my palate couldn't be questioned, and I couldn't, wouldn't adjust it to suit anyone else.

My mom cooked us fried plantains regularly, and I would eat them so quickly out of the hot oil that I'd burn my tongue. I'd still go back for more—the subtle sweetness touched by salt and fat had no equal. It was the plantains that made us Puerto Rican—the plantains and the empanadas stuffed with adobo-seasoned ground beef and stuffed Spanish olives that were among my first solid foods, apparently born with a taste for brine. Oh, and the pasteles we'd get at Christmas from my dance teacher's mom, Carmen. I liked the bites with the tiny pieces of pork the best in those. Being Puerto Rican, one has what's called la mancha de plátano—plantain stain. When frying plantains to make tostones, it's important not to spray oil on yourself: It will stain. In colloquial use, the phrase refers to a permanent marker of ethnic identity among a population who can all look remarkably different—there is no one identifiable race, hair color, or texture to assign as "Puerto Rican."

We weren't in touch with my grandmother's family, and she never wanted to go back. My father didn't seem interested in this aspect of his heritage; I can't even remember him eating the plantains. These were something my mom cooked for her children, for us to know ourselves. The plantains were all we had, until I wanted more.

—

Once in college and studying history, I noticed for maybe the first time that Puerto Rico was unique among Latin American countries for never having really gained independence. It passed from the hands of the Spanish empire to the United States' in 1898, and in the hands of the U.S. it has remained ever since, as a colony. I can remember the moment it occurred to me to look into it, at my desk in my lime-green room, doing a search on the 2005 Mac PowerBook I'd saved up for and finding the book *Puerto Rico: The Trials of the Oldest Colony in the World* by José Trías Monge. I'll never forget the cover, white with a Puerto Rican flag merging into the U.S.'s stars and stripes—disappearing into it. Here I was being radicalized by feminist poetry and the ex-Jesuit priest Marxist professor of my class on contemporary philosophy, but no one told me that Puerto Rico was a colony. We were reading post-colonial writing, as though this past were really past; here was a colony still in the present.

I had only made three trips to Puerto Rico before I returned in 2015 as a writer on assignment. They were perfunctory vacations, a little depressing. Two of them were with Todd, and for the first, we stayed at a terrible all-inclusive resort. On the second, he made me cry by suggesting we eat at Chili's while I was hoping to find some *real* food. We ended up at a crappy Argentinian spot (now closed) where the lettuce in my Caesar salad tasted of chilled refrigerator. The third was a solo trip to lie on the beach and read for a few days to reward myself for freelancing enough on top of my day job to take myself on vacation. But on one of those early trips, we had one stunning meal that included a coconut panna cotta garnished with carambola, or starfruit, and I ate a pastelillo filled with crab from a kiosk in Piñones—these were the delicious things I knew had to be here if I just knew where to find them. I got to practice the Spanish I started learning at twelve and will forever be learning. After college, I was taking continuing education classes at NYU trying, endlessly, to become fluent. But I asked for books by Álvaro Enrigue and Reinaldo Arenas at what was Librería Tertulia, a bookstore by the University of Puerto Rico's central Río Piedras campus, and was understood.

On these trips, which took place in the three years after the 2008 economic crisis, I noticed more of what was ugly in San Juan than what was beautiful. I noticed the abandoned buildings, the empty storefronts, the fact that it wasn't a given that you could go just anywhere and be served a wonderful meal of chuleta, tostones, rice and beans. In the metro area, more accommodating of tourists than beyond its boundaries, there were chain restaurants and fast food to satisfy their (our?) palates. This wasn't my magical fantasy land of Santería and abundant fruit; it was a real place suffering under the yoke of U.S. colonialism and inept local governance. Nonetheless, this ugliness was complemented by so much natural beauty, pockets of bookshops and good food, and extensive history—in my youthful gaze, there was truth here about the state of the world, of international politics and economics, in the fact that the ugliness couldn't be hidden. Never mind that with such ugliness comes pain, misery, poverty; that when the ugliness isn't fixed, it all gets worse. I know that now, but what it taught me then was that I couldn't take my perspective on things for granted. I couldn't believe anywhere in the world had only one story to tell: Life anywhere wasn't either the worst or the best. It was everything you could imagine, all at once.

—

Plantains have always been central to Puerto Rican cooking—but when I say "Puerto Rican cooking," I mean that specifically. This isn't the cooking of Borinquen, as the archipelago would've been called by its original inhabitants, but of the Spanish colonized Puerto Rico, named Rich Port for its purpose of use. They're a symbol of the national identity and its cuisine, but it's not an indigenous crop. Plantains, a relative of the banana, originated, like many tropical foodstuffs, in Southeast Asia and were brought to the Caribbean by way of Africa. They were a cheap way to feed the enslaved populations who were working the sugarcane fields. The standard plate of the Spanish Caribbean includes a starch (a vianda), a meat, and rice and beans—because this was how the enslaved were fed, to keep them alive and working in the stark sun for no money. It's remained the go-to meal.

Plantains are most often served as tostones, twice-fried and flattened, when they're green, or as amarillos (called maduros elsewhere) when yellow, which are sweet and sticky after being dropped in hot oil.

—

When I was traveling more to Puerto Rico, and even on those sad initial trips, I kept being introduced to more ways of eating plantains than I'd ever known in New York. There was mofongo, of course, which is where the plantains are fried and then mashed with chicharrones, pork skin, and garlic, topped with the protein or vegetable of your choice, usually in a saucy mix. There are also canoas, where they're kept whole but sliced vertically, stuffed, and baked. There's pastelón, a kind of lasagna with beef picadillo and cheese, where yellow sweet plantains stand in for pasta sheets. When the fruit is between green and yellow, with a skin that shows both colors, you can still make tostones, but they'll be called pintón and gently sweet, a little fluffy. *Pintón*—at first, whenever my husband would say it, I'd hear "pintao" like an abbreviation of "pintado," or painted; it made sense considering the swipe of yellow upon the green, like God took a brush to it while you had your back turned. As many things as you could imagine doing with a plantain, they're possible. Like a banana, they're useful in this hot, humid climate because even when their skin turns black and the flesh goes soft, they're edible. There's always food to be made with a plantain that serves what's available in the rest of the pantry or the leftovers in the fridge. But I like them most sliced into thin, thin, thin airy strips and eaten with pigeon peas in escabeche.

There are also many varieties of plantain, just like banana. Mafafo is short and fat, and this is the one we see most often locally as well as the traditional, which can sometimes weigh in at more than a pound when the season is right. The Hawaiian plantain is even fatter than the mafafo; both are squat—so much diversity that is lost in the translation of plant from origin to faraway supermarket or specialty grocer. Or could a mafafo become the truffle of the plantain world, if marketed just right? I don't want to consider it.

—

With my reporting trips, I liked to remain in the background as much as possible. What I wanted access to was information, yes, but more observation, the ability to observe a chef or a bartender just doing their job. I'm always going to be better at observing than reporting, a lesson of my years with social anxiety, of trying and often failing to learn how the "normal" people behaved. But people wanted to hang out a bit, have a beer, understand what my deal was, why I was interested in what was happening in San Juan or Puerto Rico broadly. Inevitably, they'd take a sideways glance at me and ask, *Are you Latin?* or I'd make some passing comment about where my grandmother was born. When it would come out that I had some of this in me—some of this Puerto Ricanness, this Boricuaness—I still didn't know what to do with it. It wasn't enough and it was diasporic, too: I realized how different Nuyoricans were from people who grew up on the archipelago, that there was tension in the local understanding of those who'd left, who didn't endure the hurricanes and the frequent blackouts. While going out for dumplings at five a.m. one morning in Condado, I watched a girl from the Bronx dressed for the club cry into her fried rice, "I'm Puerto Rican but they don't treat me like I am." If I never claimed anything, I couldn't be hurt; if I never claimed anything, it couldn't be taken away from me.

On every visit—on vacation, as a reporter—I spent time trying to figure out how much of myself could really fit in. My grandmother, Rosa, was a diasporic anomaly. She never longed for nor spoke longingly of this archipelago she left in the 1940s, while I became somewhat obsessed. I'd wave her small flag on the front lawn of her house during summers when she babysat my brother and me, and she'd yell at me to stop; it would be years later that I'd realize it was because she was trying to hide, that Puerto Rican pride could be understood as threatening to the order of empire. The rest of my ancestry being Western European means it was white, or it was assimilated into whiteness. Here, in my Puerto Ricanness, was something I couldn't disappear into; this was something I had to seek in order to claim. Because the place held no good memories for my grandmother and she didn't try to pass on much of her remembrance of it to her children or grandchildren, I had to build it. She wasn't trying to maintain any connection to the land after she left;

it was the opposite. She wanted to rid herself of it, of a place where she was an orphan with a murdered brother. Marrying my Irish-German grandfather was a way of disappearing it. I only heard her speak her native tongue when she was suffering that deep dementia. *Mentirosa.* When I fumble in my Spanish, when a driver tells me, "Tiene un acento muy raro," I figure it's her cursing me.

There were books I had to read, recipes I had to study. I've always been sheepish about what it means to be a quarter Rican; everyone understands it differently, thinks I should identify it differently. I've never felt comfortable making the call for myself. *What are you?* they ask. Indeed, what am I? Your guess is as good as mine. Could my attachment to this place be more than pastelillos and plantains if I can't dance salsa, if I don't want to perreo, if my Spanish falters?

—

When I moved to San Juan (without knowing I was moving to San Juan) in July 2019, it was just a couple of weeks before the start of what would be massive protests to oust the governor, Ricky Rosselló, after the leak of a document showing conversations between high-ranking government officials that were gross, sexist, demeaning, diminishing—they demonstrated a clear wish to make the archipelago a full-on tax haven for outsiders rather than a place where Puerto Ricans could thrive and build their lives. "I saw the future, it's so wonderful, there are no Puerto Ricans," as Edwin Miranda, a close adviser of the then-governor, wrote.

People took to the streets immediately, and the crowds swelled to a massive crescendo with a general strike and march on July 22, from Expreso Las Américas to the Fortaleza, the governor's mansion. Nightly, throughout the two weeks of intense and relentless protest, the police responded with incredible force and tear gas. The tension would grow palpable after nine p.m., hitting a peak toward eleven p.m., when we knew that the gas was coming. But the protestors would hold strong, ready with blends of Maalox and water in plastic bottles to pour over burning eyes. On my first night there, I ran and saw a girl being carried, her arms and legs flailing, because she couldn't see and was crying out. As Israel and I tried to make our way out of the mayhem, the police would catch protestors at each block and form a line before releasing more gas. It was like watching a movie, on repeat, for days. But the stinging in our eyes, the rapid beating of our hearts were real.

The day of July 24, it was said that the police were going to be even more violent and unrestrained. People still gathered at the Fortaleza. They still danced; they still sold cold water and Medalla beers. They still sang and chanted. They did perreo on the steps of the cathedral, where they taped up a trans pride flag—a sight that brought my rebellious Catholic school heart to tears. I took a break from the crowd to sit at the bar where Israel was working when I heard a girl running, her feet making such loud, excited stomping noises, down the sidewalk. "He resigned," I said out loud, not even entertaining the idea that she was running away from something. And then it came, the announcement: Ricky had resigned. Shots all around.

Was this the jump-off point of a hoped-for revolution? No. Politicians from Rosselló's PNP party, which has a somewhat incoherent political platform that is for statehood as well as deep tax breaks for foreigners' business dealings, are still in power. But the PIP, the Independence Party, gained ground in the 2020 elections and again in 2024, receiving more of the vote than they'd ever gotten before.

There are many reasons it is so difficult for Puerto Ricans, for Puerto Rico, to put a stop to the colonial situation. It's never been a decision that locals have been able to vote for in any binding way, and there are so many structural, historical, and cultural barriers to self-determination.

The refrain of visitors, "Why doesn't Puerto Rico just become a state?" as though that's such a simple thing, as though that's actually a desirable thing, is exhausting. Usually these visitors have no clue of the extent to which their United States has put its thumb on the possibility of a liberated Puerto Rico through the active suppression of any potential leaders for independence, such as Pedro Albizu Campos. They don't know about the Ponce Massacre of 1937 or the gag law that made it illegal to display the Puerto Rican flag from 1948 to 1957. They don't know that Lolita Lebrón went into the Capitol in 1954 and opened fire, yelling "Viva Puerto Rico libre!" and said, while being arrested, "I did not come to kill anyone. I came to die for Puerto Rico!" They don't know that Filiberto Ojeda Ríos, another independence activist, was shot dead in his own home in 2005. They don't know of the "carpetas," the FBI's files on anyone known for nationalist activities. Maybe they don't even know that in 2016, President Barack Obama put in place a fiscal control board known colloquially as "la junta," which has put austerity measures in place and controls the economy: big, juicy checks for those who manage it while 40 percent of the population lives in poverty.

These sorts of reasons were, on top of the personal, familial loss she suffered, why my grandmother couldn't feel connected to this ancestry, wanted to be far from it, didn't want her children or grandchildren to know it in any real way. To her, it wasn't worthwhile. Puerto Rico gave her nothing, that's true. I know so many people of the diaspora whose parents, grandparents, were present, wanted them to know about where they came from, wanted them to spend summers with family on the archipelago, wanted them to know the recipes, the music, the culture. I envy them as I envy the stories of my own ancestors who came from what I believed to be more exciting places.

I've reverse-engineered my connection, but I'm not sure it will ever feel less confusing. This is the burden of diaspora, of mixed identity, and I also see it as the gift. I have to work to define myself and who I am; I don't have the privilege of seeing the world just one way. I see the world through a prism. It used to be that when people suggested I was writing about Puerto Rican food because of my heritage, I would shut them down. "No, no—it's about politics," I'd say. "It's about food sovereignty, that's my interest. I'm not on some big repatriation journey, no, of course not."

And it was, of course. I had spent years writing about vegan food that could be found despite the island cuisine's "meaty" reputation, about the women who were part of a very male-centric culinary scene, and the ways in which operations like Huerto Rico were trying to create something new for the archipelago's food culture. I was visiting farms like Frutos del Guacabo and the distillery of Don Q to hear about goat milk and generating power out of water waste (respectively). I was looking for the ways a place so battered by disasters both human-made and natural could find new ways to feed itself, to create, because I did and do believe that the affluent nations of the world that are actually responsible for climate change can learn from this kind of survival. Not resilience, as so many people call it, trying to put a nice face on what is done to withstand colonization and the boot of empire. No, it's survival—straight up, against the odds and against the desires of those who wield power, influence, money. Puerto Rico endures so much ugliness and always emerges beautiful: How? I'll be asking this question for the rest of my life.

—

I got my Caribbean writer life, by way of curiosity about an ancestry, grit, and accidental love. I see the ocean every day, and I sweat while I work. Like New York City, it's also given me exactly what I knew it would: fresh perspective and experiences that have changed and shaped my writing. Plantains are seasonal, did you know? I didn't. The tropics aren't just one thing, either. They have many seasons, many terrains, many microclimates.

While I'd had this knowledge of the sugar, coffee, bananas, and chocolate that we got in the global north being from elsewhere, needing safeguarding in the way of regulations like fair trade to ensure decent working and farming conditions because they couldn't be guaranteed, here I see the abandoned sugar mills on drives. Here I see the diversity of bananas and plantains that are possible when the market demands of monocrops aren't fed—when, instead, the needs of the land are respected. I see cacao trees providing shade for coffee bushes. I wonder whether I should get some cacao for myself when it's at the farmers' market and ferment it, grind it, do my own bean to bar experimentation.

Life here isn't the kind of fantasy I had—the fantasy where I'd make my own chocolate and always have plantains to eat. It's difficult to obtain necessities without a car, and we don't own one. Tourists are everywhere, all the time, and they don't move from the corners: They stand there and gawk, take pictures, as though they're on the "It's a Small World" ride and not taking up space in a real place. Mi acento es muy raro, and so people often switch to English once I open my mouth, meaning my Spanish stays preserved in its post-collegiate amber. I start to study French.

I like it, though, even the difficulties—not always in the day to day, but in the aggregate. To live here is to always be wrestling with that duality of ugliness and beauty that defines the human experience, turned up loud. The economy sucks but I can always find someone to say hello to down in the plaza. The little things mean more; they add up to more. I've always been wrestling with that in my own mind, I realize: My life has been so good and so bad, all at once. So dull and too exciting, in the wrong ways, in volatile, violent, and miserable ways. My family was the type to have red-capped whole milk in the fridge, and I would also study my father's work schedule, stuck to it with a magnet, to see which weeks he wouldn't be home in the evenings and we could breathe. No wonder I like to focus on words and ingredients, with their clear meanings and purpose. Aside from the occasional cliché or oven burn, they don't hurt me. They're a way to navigate the world. They're the escape hatch I grew up longing for and sought, misguidedly, in a boy turned man.

—

To be Puerto Rican gave me plantains and a desire to come to the place where I would meet the love of my life; to be Puerto Rican gave me the feeling that I'd never really be fully anything, never find any real roots, and connected me to ancestral pain and erasure rooted in my grandmother. I have thought that living here would provide clarity about my identity, about what I can or should claim, and it's given me some of that, but mostly it's given me necessary perspective, that setting I longed for, the sweat of a good edit. Life isn't a movie where ghosts speak or where you heal generational curses, but

I've fixed something within myself and know more ways to cook a plantain than I ever could've imagined. My tostones have gotten so much better: smashed to near paper thinness, uniformly fried in coconut oil, dusted with flaky salt, and sprinkled with scallions for a touch of freshness.

On Sugar

During my vegan bakery year, I would order my ingredients from a natural foods distributor based in Queens. They only delivered to the pirate kitchen of my apartment because it was upstairs from a karate studio and a witchcraft shop, so I could pretend that I didn't live upstairs—it was just my kitchen. I would haul the fifty-pound sacks of fair-trade sugar—crystal, powdered, brown—and New York–grown and milled flour up the stairs, then empty them into plastic Cambro containers. Huge restaurant-size cans of coconut milk and buckets of coconut oil were in my orders, too. The chocolate I ordered directly from the manufacturer, and I made sure to get the baking discs in at least two varieties of sweetness—a 60 percent cacao, a 70 percent cacao, one for cookies and the other for ganache. My home kitchen in Huntington Village was made industrial to serve the local appetite for vegan chocolate-chunk cookies, marzipan pops, coconut cupcakes filled with chocolate ganache, and pumpkin cakes with walnut buttercream.

That local appetite for vegan sweets was big enough to take over my refrigerator and a lot of floor space, but it wasn't really that big. One of the things running a microbakery taught me was that food service in general relies on an extraordinary bounty of ingredients. Chocolate was my way into understanding global foodways, and sugar—the utter excess of it that was required, like 300 grams of powdered sugar for one batch of American-style stiff buttercream—really drove home the sinister nature of those foodways. Sugar, friend of chocolate: There's no way to have its specific sweetness without exploitation, is there?

—

These are the knots I'm always trying to untie, and it's why the baker I was influenced the writer I became. All things considered, it shouldn't have surprised me that the writer I became eventually found herself a food studies professor walking through sugarcane fields of an old plantation under hot sun: I went from hauling sacks of it up the stairs to demonstrating how it tells the story of colonial exploitation of people and land for a group of gastronomy students. Some of them simply wanted to eat tostones, but to consider the plantain—symbol of Puerto Rican culinary culture born in Southeast Asia, which made its way to these shores via Africa and Spanish colonizers—is to also consider sugar, which made a similar journey.

I'd been asked to teach a culinary tourism class that included bringing my students on a weeklong trip around the archipelago. Rather than give a feel-good course about the power of food to connect us (that power might account for 10 percent of the full story, in my view), I wanted to root culinary tourism in its economic, colonial, and agricultural realities, both historic and contemporary. We'd toured Casa Pueblo, a nonprofit in the southwestern mountain town of Adjuntas focused on energy independence; visited the indoor farmers' market at Plaza Mercado de Río Piedras and the outdoor lechón purveyors of Guavate; and one day was spent completely focused on the history of sugar locally. As a baker and a writer who'd downed her fair share of rum (always number two in my heart, after gin), this history was utterly fascinating to me: Every time Israel and I drove around the island, I wanted to go see the nearest abandoned sugarcane refinery. They dotted the entire verdant landscape—metal graveyards memorializing a loss that was also sort of a gain, considering the back-breaking work and who was forced to do it—creating a tangible reminder of where all that sweet stuff had come from and how massive an aspect of the local economy it had once been.

The first order of business on the former plantation tour is to walk right into the sugarcane field, to feel the height and weight of this thick grass—to understand that it could cut you. Hot sun relentlessly beat down on us, unimpeded by shade. "Imagine hacking through this with a machete," said the tour guide at Hacienda La Esperanza in Manatí, on the north coast of Puerto Rico. She was dressed for the outdoors, a sleek female Indiana Jones in well-tailored khaki and a wide-brimmed hat with a cord under her neck to keep it from blowing away in the wind. Cutting the cane would have been excruciatingly difficult labor; this was obvious from just looking at it. This labor was almost always performed by the enslaved.

The excruciating reality of this back-breaking labor is what we are meant to understand before we go into the house, where we can see how large and heavy the machetes are as they hang rusted on a spinning circular rack. We also read the letters of the enslaved who tried to seek justice for their plight from the very Spaniards who put them in their bleak position. A manual sugarcane press was still there on the property, restored so that one could see how much work it took to get the cane from field to press and then onto whatever function the sugar would serve. Crystals came to be made white, unstained by the remnants of molasses, through filtering with bone char made from animal remnants. Brown sugar would retain some molasses stickiness, while molasses itself—considered a by-product—would be distilled into rum. There were 789 sugar haciendas around Puerto Rico at the height of the industry in the nineteenth century, and in the 1940s, there were seventeen rum distilleries. Now there are two major rum houses—Bacardi and Serralles, which makes Don Q—and some smaller operations. The largest two import molasses; there are no large-scale operational sugarcane refineries left on the island. In 2000, the last one closed, adding itself to the ledger of ghosts of agrarian pasts.

We went from Hacienda la Esperanza's perspective on the history of sugarcane that centers the experience of the enslaved laborers—of trying to feel, despite the impossibility, its real brutality—over to San Juan Artisan Distillers, which does grow its own sugarcane and distill small-batch rums called Ron Pepón from the juice. This is a different style than most Puerto Rican rums and is more akin to the French-style of rhum agricole. Not using molasses makes for a grassier, earthier flavor—the terroir of the cane remains, though because of sugarcane's history, one wonders how valuable such a terroir should be.

At the distillery, the tour guide was fitted with a small microphone and sunnily told us that the men in the tall, grassy fields were cutting the cane "the traditional way" with machetes—here the brutality is reframed as the human touch that makes the rum better. This is the way of artisanal goods in the twenty-first century. I nervously ask her how often they're allowed breaks, considering the experience we'd just had. She assures us that it's every hour.

—

Given that I organized this sugarcane immersion day, it would make sense that this dichotomy reflected precisely what makes sugar so endlessly fascinating to me: Most of us only know the sweetness of it because of the brutality of colonialism and slavery; we, or some of us, keep trying to find a way to small-batch our way into better sugar and thus better rum. A sugar, a rum that we can feel good about that retains the brilliance of our nostalgia while acknowledging the immiseration of their true origins.

The artisanal shift in the conversation around food—the one that made me the person I am, the vegan baker with the local flour, fair-trade chocolate and sugar, the hope for a taste of nostalgia without the corporate and historic baggage—is all about some kind of restoration but with the education of hindsight. How much it's really making a dent in the way things are done is the question that looms.

Any thoughtful person who is in the business of bulk-buying ingredients is going to ask themselves about how much of an effect they're really having on the way things are done. To haul sacks of sugar and flour up the stairs, pour them into massive containers, and then wipe them off your hands over and over on your apron invites these kinds of questions. This was on the mind of my friend, the bread-baker and pâtissier Diego San Miguel, when he called me out of the blue one afternoon. He's a baker and wanted to know, could we host a sugar tasting—is it even possible? "A cupping," he said, like they do with coffee to understand its nuances.

Not possible—there wasn't enough variety, and if there were, it wasn't being sold in Puerto Rico, where the sugar on the shelves was imported and then packaged up as Dulce Caña or Snow White. There are many other styles of sugar from the granulated one that is so commonly understood, used, and called for in most Western recipes. Jaggery, from India, for instance, is similar to what's called panela and piloncillo in Latin America: they're blocks of brown sweetener where sugarcane juice is boiled and poured into molds. There is sap from date or toddy palms mixed into jaggery, too. There are dates; there's honey and agave syrup, maple syrup; there's sorghum. But more than anything, when it comes to what most folks think of when they hear the words "sugar" or "sweetener," there are the crystals derived from the grass full of sucrose known as sugarcane.

Diego and I agreed that heirloom sugar could be the next big thing, though, now that grain has had its own renaissance, following in coffee's wake thanks to a sourdough surge and restored interest in regional grains. "Sugar is stuck in the nineties," he said. In terms of hip ingredients having their day in the artisanal sun, he's right. Fair-trade sugar, in which a third party approves a company's business and ecological practices, is still a niche sector, as with chocolate or bananas. It's the kind of label that either piques interest or is glossed over in a hurried run through the grocery store. That these labels always come with a heftier price tag doesn't help.

—

The Spanish colonizers first brought saccharum to the Caribbean with the second voyage of Columbus in 1493, and it would gradually become a significant aspect of local agriculture. Its history in Puerto Rico has been marked by various major events throughout the centuries. There were periods of prosperity, and the first significant surge occurred between 1790 and 1849. These measures partially revoked the Spanish monopoly on commerce, which allowed for easier trade with other nations but also allowed enslaved people to work the land. Following the Haitian Revolution in 1791, demand for Puerto Rican sugar in the United States increased.

The most significant text on the role of sugar to be written is Sidney W. Mintz's *Sweetness and Power: The Place of Sugar in Modern History*, originally published in 1985. He writes about how sugar entered the diets of Europeans and became the ubiquitous if un-diverse commodity we have grown accustomed to having available at our fingertips. Mintz did fieldwork in Puerto Rico in the middle of the twentieth century, publishing *Worker in the Cane: A Puerto Rican Life History* in 1960. He references that experience in the first pages of *Sweetness and Power*: "...the sugar was not being produced for the Puerto Ricans themselves: they consumed only a fraction of the finished product." Most of it went to Seville, Spain, and then it went to Boston. The sugar always served the empire, like other crops. That's how it's come to be that Puerto Rico imports 80 percent of its food, including the sugar it once grew in such robust quantities.

With Operation Bootstrap, put in place in the 1940s after the U.S. had come to be the archipelago's colonizer, agriculture was undermined, and the rise of factories caused an exodus to the cities. From the implementation of that plan to now, one sees its effects on food in Puerto Rico, and sugar was symbolic of that, on the archipelago with only the rusted ruins of mills standing in vast fields or, such as on Vieques, overrun already by plant life. In the twenty-first century, there has been political turmoil, economic collapse, and crumbling infrastructure while the reliance on imported food in supermarkets has made groceries wildly expensive. Diminishing the role of agriculture and the cultural figure of the farmer has had catastrophic effects, though younger people are returning to the land more and more, having learned firsthand what happens in a disaster when one is dependent on outside sources of food.

Sugar still has a significant cultural role locally even if its market share has been depleted. A farmer I talk to every weekend occasionally brings some cut cane, and when I ask, she tells me they have two kinds that grow "like weeds," and they'll sometimes open them up to suck on the sticky innards for a snack. In mountain towns, there is still a strong culture of making pitorro, a clandestine rum distilled on a small scale from sugarcane juice that persists despite the local and international rum industry (and its questionable legality). During Christmastime, orders are made for bottles flavored with passion fruit, ginger, and tamarind. Guarapo, an unfermented sugarcane juice, is sold locally in plastic cups or jugs, and it's even made into a beer by local Ocean Lab Brewing. But San Juan Artisan Distillers, which replanted sugarcane in order to make their Ron Pepón, remains the only operation working in an organized, aboveboard way, and it can still only be a small-batch product if it wants to retain cachet.

Like coffee, sugar had become a symbol of local agrarian life. Unlike in coffee, where baristas and café owners have led a charge for transparency and direct trade with farmers, there is perhaps not enough demand for fostering old diversity in sugar crops and creating new avenues for supporting farmers, who could—in some potential future—sell premium, small-batch sugar while also growing food for subsistence and locals. I have been simultaneously frustrated and awed when I see these mills, because I want to eat from the land on which I live and support its tending, its laborers. But I am also bourgeois and selfish: I know fresher sugar would taste better, that a small-batch ingredient like this would add a new dimension to my baking. In a globalized world, the local retains magic so long as one can afford it.

This is the double-edged sword of this taste in artisanal food, of the desire to make a cupcake or a pie with the most pristine ingredients money can buy: Who's at the source of each of these, and can they pay their bills? Can the bakers pay their bills if they want to get the best ingredients?

Vanilla, another ingredient so crucial to my precious baking project, is so labor intensive to grow that it's a wonder there is any at all. When I get a local vanilla bean and I can see the tiny black spots of its inner paste whipped into chilled coconut cream and a tablespoon of powdered sugar for lightness: The satisfaction I feel is not just aesthetic or gastronomic or political—it's all of the above. But I don't know how much it means. "Every ingredient here was grown in Puerto Rico," I will say, placing a vegan chocolate pudding—made like tembleque, a coconut pudding, where melted chocolate, coconut milk, and cornstarch are gently heated over the stove and then chilled to a smooth, jiggling finish—topped with that whipped cream on the table for dessert. I'll mean the vanilla, chocolate, and coconut milk, but the sugar? It will have been imported. It's left out of my mental calculations, just like the cornstarch, for being insignificant to the end result: invisible except for the necessary sweetness and structure. Can sweetness come to the foreground and be as important as the vanilla and chocolate? I'm not fermenting and grinding cacao, but I'd love to squeeze some sugarcane. Or maybe I'd just like to drink a mojito with Ron Pepón, to get as close as I can to it.

My obsessive focus on origins earns wide eyes of shock, because only I have the time and professional excuses to care this much. All my guests will care about is how it tastes, and I guess that's the most important part of my job in those moments: making the background, the origins deliciously invisible. Part of serving a delectable dish will always be about obscuring the labor, which is maybe why it's so important to me never to do the same while writing. If we ever learn to value sugar and all these other ingredients central to our most joyful traditions, the land they're grown on, the labor of the people who work it, and the fruits of their existence in our kitchens, it will mean that we have created a whole new world.

—

Looking at abandoned mills around the Puerto Rican archipelago requires mourning, but it's not the industry that is to be mourned: it's the lives and the potential for a different world untouched by the exploitation of slavery, colonization, and capitalism. We don't know how we would eat without the sugar industry; we can't say for sure we'd rely on regional sweeteners, like honey or agave or sorghum. But it is in acknowledging sugar's bitter past that we can imagine a sweeter future for all. I like to think about that farmer, who thinks nothing of the sugarcane on her land that grows wild like a weed. I like to think about that sugarcane itself, growing tall for its own sake. I like to think of my friend Diego, the baker, who keeps wondering about different possible futures. Considering the connections from the kitchen to the field are for those of who are doing the work. Everyone else's job is to enjoy the end result, and maybe ask a question that will open up a new way of seeing their food. Each chocolate bar, sweetened by sugar, has that potential to be a portal.

On Pumpkin

"I WISH WE WERE APPLYING THESE IDEAS SOMEWHERE less colonial," a student said to me after the tour at Hacienda la Esperanza. We were eating at a small restaurant in a strip mall before we went to the distillery. On our plates were plantains, rice and beans, and—for most of the students but not me—some kind of meat. This was the standard plate of comida criolla—the Puerto Rican cuisine that is a blend of indigenous, Spanish, and African influence—meant to help someone spend their day in the hot sun laboring, likely with a machete in hand.

I didn't know what to say about this comment that wouldn't be insulting, though I understood the sentiment: There was a lot to take in, and if interpreted in a specific way, there was a lot to feel guilty about. One can either approach the complications and horrors of history with an openness to learn, or the overwhelming nature of all that came before will make one want to turn away. Some people will just want the chocolate pudding, please, without the backstory; others will find the backstory enhances every note of the cacao, its bitterness enriched by the smoky hit of the vanilla bean worked into light, luscious cream.

As I shrugged off the comment that I found both understandable and ignorant, perhaps my tight-lipped smile told the whole story playing out in my mind. I looked down at my plate for a way to change the subject and noticed a chunk of orange in my beans, and so I parlayed the conversation away from the colonial status of Borinquen and said, "This is how you know the beans are good."

It was easier to focus on the bright spot of orange in my habichuelas than give my lectures all over again. I'd learned about pumpkin being used in beans from my friend César, a great cook and child of the diaspora who grew up in Williamsburg, Brooklyn. His grandparents left Puerto Rico around the same time as my grandmother, and they brought with them a lot of old-school ways of doing things that were lost to time even on the island itself as convenience took over as far more fashionable than making food from scratch.

He'd always complimented the beans at Walmart's cafeteria for this, and it was just likely that someone there in the kitchen preferred the old way of doing things. Chunks of pumpkin, or calabaza, would be put in with the pink kidney beans in order to thicken the sauce with its starch—and I'm sure the extra nutrition helped with filling people up during lean times.

The way I'd structured the class was to explicitly center

Puerto Rico: its colonial history, its resistance, and the ways in which its economic structure was inevitably set up for locals to be put in subservient positions to tourists. I didn't know another way to teach the class, considering I had friends and neighbors who were being displaced to make room for Airbnbs, and Israel and I were feeling the squeeze at the supermarket, where imported goods that had been made more pricey because of inflation were even more expensive because of legislation that doesn't allow the colony to trade directly with anyone but the U.S. (why the Spanish garlic or Canadian onions would be moldy by the time they got to us). Every essential aspect of life was rigged to benefit corporations or the U.S., and living here made that exploitation part of the air I breathed. My frustrations over time were becoming amplified: Why should I smile at people who are leaving their mojito cups on my stoop for me to clean up? Why be polite to those who ask me to take their picture by shoving a phone into my hands and not saying thank you? Living somewhere that visitors don't treat as a "real place"—this takes its toll. In teaching this class, I was able to restore some power, some dignity, to the story of how food has a role to play—both positive and negative—in these dynamics of travel.

The plantation to paradise pipeline is a narrative and transition familiar to many Caribbean islands. They were once used for their natural resources, which were extracted and shipped back to the head of the empire, and now they were meant to serve as entertainment and escape for the residents of those imperial centers. Puerto Rico and these other islands—they're the periphery, inconsequential and made for use. When I've complained about how tourists clog the sidewalks of Old San Juan, I've been told, "Well, you live in the tourist center." Yes, the tourist center—that natural rock formation, that place where it's every visitor's God-given right to make a ruckus. Israel grew up here, just around the corner from where we live now. Somehow, he's not as real as those people visiting for just a weekend and screaming as they drink their way down the streets.

—

Calabaza is everywhere in Puerto Rico: It grows everywhere, in every microclimate, and chefs use it in so many ways, both savory and sweet. I've had it cold and marinated as a carpaccio, as filling in an eggplant lasagna, and baked with a stuffing of zucchini that has effectively melted down into a cream. At home, I'm often steaming it in chunks that I can feed the dog as both treat and bellyache remedy, or that I'll spice and season to purée and mix in with labneh for my own enjoyment. The tang of the strained yogurt meets the warm earthiness of the squash and goes perfectly on top of a crunchy slice of toasted sourdough. With a garnish of toasted, salty squash seeds for crunch? An exquisite lunch.

Pumpkin was pie for me growing up on Long Island, where the namesake Long Island cheese pumpkin has been prized, its seeds saved, and is named for looking like a rind of aged dairy. The first time I cooked pumpkin was back in Huntington, when I roasted one myself for pie. I went to Whole Foods and chose a pumpkin, marked on its signage with the "local" imprimatur. It was a pretty pale orange, with deep, wide ridges, and it was a bit squat—a squat squash, like a garden elf had sat on it during its development. Stunning, though—elegant and unlike the loud bright orange pumpkins with thin shallow ridges of October picking. It was clear these were of different stock, bred for different purposes—indeed, they were a different species. This Whole Foods squash looked to me like a North Shore pumpkin: a rich girl with a Longchamp bag.

After slicing it in half, removing the seeds and stringy gunk, I roasted the halves face down until easily pierced with a fork. Then I scooped out the cooked flesh and made the purée in the food processor. I had no clue what I was doing, really, and the purée wasn't as dense as what you find in a can. There was too much water. Now I know: It needed to be left to drain in a cheesecloth. I could've just bought organic pumpkin purée—which is usually butternut squash—in a can. But I was so stubborn, and so committed, and through that stupidity and misguided commitment to an ill-defined integrity, I learned my lessons.

I'd eaten pumpkin pie during the holidays growing up: It was a favorite of mine, as I preferred all cream pies to fruit ones. Hot, gelatinous fruit in a flaky crust didn't do it for me. A custard did. When I started to bake, I figured it was my duty to make pumpkin pie and to do it in a way that was my own. One of the other lessons I learned, aside from the one about the liquid content of fresh squash, was that I didn't need to reinvent the wheel with every recipe. Some things are classic as they are, and even if you make them vegan, it's okay if they just satisfy some old nostalgic urge.

That local variety of pumpkin I had picked out at Whole Foods, known in Latin as *Cucurbita moschata*, is indigenous to the Americas and had become well known in the 1800s; it was mentioned frequently in cookbooks of the time, but it was falling out of fashion until a seed saver named Ken Ettlinger revived its popularity in the 1970s through the Long Island Seed Project. By the time the local food movement was rip-roaring in the early 2000s, when I started to get interested in food, the Long Island cheese pumpkin was experiencing a renaissance and an extensive press run. It didn't just have looks on its side, though: There was and is substance. When they sell pumpkins for cooking on Long Island at the supermarket outside the autumn season, it's going to be marked "tropical calabasa" or "calabasa Jamaican" at Meat Farms or just "calabaza" at H Mart. The Caribbean pumpkin has a year-long presence now and is easy to find because of demographic shifts.

These are the same calabazas that are common in Puerto Rico, and they're of the same cultivar as the Long Island cheese pumpkin, *Cucurbita moschata*—they were grown all over the hemisphere, spreading with people and knowledge, and became known for holding up to hot, humid climates as well as disease. I always think of the crawling vine of the pumpkin, dotted with bright yellow flowers, as a vein connecting my island homes. In pumpkin, I don't have to choose. This is a rare case.

—

Apples, that other common pie filling, haven't been so easy. They, along with pumpkins, signal fall for me: one for its season, the other for its cultural role and emergence in both dessert and as beloved beers served in pint glasses with cinnamon-sugar rims. Changes in the weather have made it so that I'm often taking my first pumpkin beer of the season outdoors, swatting bees away from my glass.

In my tropical home, I've longed to taste the temperate. When did I even start to think about apples? It was when I started to crave them the way I'd once longed for tropical fruit: bananas, mangoes, coconuts, pineapples. I never considered the apple until I was desperate to eat one, and there weren't any local varieties to be found. I poured my desire into other fruits and vegetables, and pumpkin became the main one.

Pumpkin grows so well here that a farmer I know tells me she often boils chunks of it while cooking other things, then serves it simply with olive oil and salt. Its ubiquity, I realize, is probably the real reason it always ends up in the beans. My husband asks for the flowers of the pumpkin—flor de calabaza or squash blossoms, as my mom always called them.

I've shown him how you can stuff them with cheese, bread them in seasoned panko, and give them a fry. My mom used to make them every summer, but she never stuffed them with cheese—we weren't a cheesy home; dairy was used judiciously. I could also simply sauté them or add them to a tart. I could put them in a quesadilla. These flowers could become new fruit. Instead, we turn them into something else entirely. The pumpkin and its blossoms become my taste of temperate home in tropical environs.

One day, pumpkin on the brain while shopping at Bonnie Slotnick's cookbook store in the East Village, I found a *Gourmet* magazine from 2007 that focused on Latin American cooking. There's a whole feature on Puerto Rican food, and I was shocked to find a platter of thinly sliced pumpkin, roasted and served with a wedge of lime. That was certainly some recipe developer's whim, because lime, while present for short seasons, is not a staple of local cuisine outside of its role in cocktail and dive bars. Acidity is needed for a lot of quite rich dishes, but in that case, one would look for pique, a blend of hot peppers and herbs in vinegar that is the go-to hot sauce. Regardless, the pumpkin being included here in such a basic preparation warmed my heart: Beautiful, shocking orange on the plate is stunning in a photo, of course, against deep blue and rich brown, but it's also true to the squash's role as something you throw on the stove or into the oven because it's there, because it grows well—so why not? Another dish for the table, something to round out the meal.

In this way, pumpkin reminds me of apples—of the bushels of them that used to make my mom sigh in the fall. If something grows well, you simply figure out what to do with it, boredom and overwhelm be damned. I had always taken apples for granted, though, and when I moved to San Juan right before the pandemic, I expected to be so overwhelmed by selections of tropical fruit that I would forget all about the fruit of my childhood; it would be everyday awe at the mangoes dropping from a tree on our morning dog walk and thrills at finding one that hadn't been burrowed into by a chango, the mischievous local black bird who had a hunger that could never be satisfied. And yes, I loved the mangoes. But eventually I started to crave the distinct feeling of my front teeth piercing the taut apple skin and finding the unique blend of acid and sweet inside. No amount of mangoes could suffice, and I couldn't eat them like an apple, anyway; I'm allergic to a toxin on their inner skin and have broken out into itchy, scaly rashes whenever I've tried. This inability to suck the flesh and juice from a mango is a strike against my belonging in the Caribbean.

A farmer at the Saturday market—the same one who boils chunks of pumpkins and has sugarcane growing like a weed—would tell me about her different varieties of bananas, and one was called "guineo manzano" for having the slightly firm texture of an apple and having some of that tart smack Thoreau had so desired. It is a delicious banana and having more than just the Cavendish variety to eat will always be thrilling, but it's no apple. She also sells carambola four for a dollar when they're in season, which are juicier and more citrus than apples; they suited me for a while, and I kept baking them in Claudia Fleming's caramel to approximate a tarte tatin. Eventually, they would no longer do. The least common tropical substitute would be the pomarrosa—the texture was correct, so dense and firm; while tart, it is wildly floral. One begins to understand, when eating or sniffing a fresh pomarrosa, why apples and roses are considered part of the same botanical family. Here, they are one.

In my Caribbean apple craving, there was the inevitable: Home for me would always require a sacrifice. *Ni de aquí, ni de allá* goes the common refrain of diaspora, but I'm diasporic by degrees: daughter of many, heir to none. Child of assimilation; child of ancestral annihilation. Only pumpkin is the bridge.

The tropical fruits that could never suffice as an apple replacement—the carambola, the pomarrosa, the free-falling mangoes, the sweet acid of passion fruit—all smelled divine to me. "Come, sniff!" I'll say to my husband, who doesn't harbor the same fascination as I do with fresh produce, but he will kindly oblige. When my mom and sister visit, I shove fruit into their faces and command them to inhale. The craving for an apple always hits me with a jolt—an interlude in a life otherwise happy to be accommodated by the local. As a baker, I never even made them into pie, and if I'd never made them into pie, maybe I didn't love apples as much as pumpkin after all. I show my adoration and perform my fruit worship with sugar. And so I'm back to where I started: appreciating the diversity and ubiquity of this round squash that lends itself so well to fairy tales.

—

Those adventures had begun with flaky crusts, but I found my footing and my flavoring in a pumpkin cake that I served with a walnut butter buttercream back when I had the microbakery. I liked the idea of pumpkin, spiced with my blend of cinnamon, cloves, ginger, and coriander—heavy on cloves to set it apart from cloying Starbucks syrup, with the coriander there to add a hit of brightness—set against the fat nutty richness of a sweet walnut cream. I made the walnut butter by putting whole walnuts into the food processor and pulsing until they released their oil and turned into a rich paste; then I blended that with my coconut oil butter and organic powdered sugar. There would still be flecks of walnut skin visible, making it rustic and clearly made from scratch. The pumpkin cake beneath was a deep orange; the spices were spread throughout. It was a defining cupcake for me, a realization of focus: I could imagine a flavor and create it, through knowledge and a little work and some math.

Just one-quarter cup of pumpkin purée replaces an egg in baking. It performs the function of binding in that bright-orange cake, whereas in the cream filling of a pumpkin pie, it serves as flavor: The silken tofu gives the custard texture and lift that one expects of eggs in pie. Using agar, the seaweed-derived gelatin, turns pumpkin purée simmered with sugar, spices, coconut milk, and vanilla into something almost flan-like—maybe it's pudding, maybe it's panna cotta. When recipes are veganized, they become something completely different from what the language of traditional baking connotes, and I always worry about disappointing someone who's waiting for a bite that tastes *just like* the "real" thing.

Learning how to do vegan baking was an act of trial and error that goes on and on. One has to go to the edge of the imagination at first to learn where to pull back: When is it worthwhile to roast the pumpkin yourself, and when should you just use a can? Where is silken tofu going to do a better job than agar? I had taken from Thomas Keller's *Ad Hoc at Home* so much guidance, and when I started to really develop my own recipes, like the pumpkin cake, I went to Michael Ruhlman's *Ratio*—and I still do. I like to know how much I can pull back on all-purpose flour to gain flavor from almond meal (usually 20 percent) and if I'd never known how much liquid was in a large egg (two ounces), I never could've made my life-changing chocolate-chunk cookie.

This was how baking made me confident, how it built me anew into an adult who felt her agency and autonomy blooming: ingredient by ingredient, recipe by recipe, lesson by lesson. Instead of constraining me, getting into the kitchen had made me anew. The pumpkin cake and its walnut buttercream were a game-changer then, and in San Juan,

I've added completely new dimensions to how I understand it as an ingredient—how it can be the center of a dish, either in the beans or combined with sofrito to fill a pastelillo. It's not just sweet, but savory. It is still giving me the confidence and knowledge that I can use to shift a conversation toward beauty rather than ugliness. After the students and I finished our lunch, I ordered the pumpkin flan and encouraged the table to do the same.

On Grapes

THE LOVE STORY WITH ISRAEL WASN'T AS EASY AS I PRESENTED it to be. I always want to wrap my decisions in parchment paper like a block of brownies and tie them up with a nice bow of baker's twine. Over and over, I want life to be easier and tidier than it is, and over and over I learn the lesson that it will never be neat. The new beginnings I've been granted are a blessing, though they rarely feel like godsends in the moment. When I called Brian once on my way to work while I was still copyediting, walking down Canal Street and not interested in another day in a cubicle, he reminded me that I was an adult: "Man up," he said. I stood up straight from my mental breakdown and laughed. In hindsight, his tone of voice sounded shook by the idea that his older sister didn't always like the life she'd been building for herself, even once I moved to Brooklyn. When I find myself hunched over by life, I call up his voice in my head: "Man up." Again, I laugh.

This time that I had to man up, though, was when I'd had a plan to finally, really—really this time!—be a free woman. There were plans in place. My Brooklyn apartment had been packed up and driven out in a U-Haul to the garage in Patchogue. That coming September, I'd be going on a press trip to the Cognac region of France; there would be two days for me to prance around Paris before I'd go on to Madrid, where I'd drink sherry from dusty barrels and have my fill of complimentary potato chips. After that, I figured some other invitation or flight of fancy would take me on my way again. *Peripatetic* was the word, yes—this was the inspiration. I'd map my vegetarian–Bourdain posture onto more cities, learn how to read the menus in more languages, and maybe find new lovers. Who knows! I would man up, as a woman of the world.

After Israel and I had spent a nice few days together that July in San Juan, I got cold feet: People in a small industry in a small city talk a lot, and it freaked me out. For a week, I didn't talk to him nor watch his stories on Instagram: if, as a teenager in the early '00s, we told our stories of crushes and heartache through AIM, in our millennial thirties of arrested development, we were searching lists of viewers for specific avatars that might signal love, or at least a modicum of lust.

Performing my digital disinterest wasn't enough. I needed another way to prove my independence, to prove I wasn't immediately smitten and done for, and so I went out on a date with someone else. It was so much like pulling teeth to try to muster up some chemistry between me and this guy that I got home at three a.m. and immediately texted Israel: "I still have your wine." I was playing games for no reason, when I knew I wanted to be with this curly-haired bartender with a ridiculous mustache. There was no lover or European city that would have kept me from wondering, for the rest of my life, whether I should've just gotten over myself and taken this chance. "It's a booty call," a friend warned me, but I called it a declaration of love—or at least a surrender to its possibility. He was awake, of course, still working, still making mojitos for drunk tourists. Though he probably should have because of my random icy behavior, he didn't ignore me. From the next day, we were living together. We ran from the tear gas of Ricky Renuncia for two weeks, our relationship forged in this historic protest.

In all prior relationships, romantic or platonic, I'd privileged shorthand over having to explain myself: I used movie quotes and band references to stand in for real communication; I never learned how to declare my needs, so I never did. With Israel, there has been no such shorthand. Our native tongues are different, and so are our cultural touchstones. I've slowly gotten him into *Seinfeld*; he's brought me back into an appreciation of goofy Adam Sandler movies that transcend all difference. But we do actually have to talk to each other, explain ourselves to each other, and this isn't always the easiest work—neither of us grew up necessarily reveling in explaining our feelings to those around us; this didn't usually feel safe, in my case, or normal, in his. I'm not sure I know many people who did. There's a lot of watery emotion in this household (me Scorpio; he Pisces), where we live in sight of the ocean, and thus discussion must be had. I've taken to it more easily than he has: I'd been waiting my whole life not to hide my feelings and ask someone else to do things for me without fear of ridicule or rage! I'd been waiting my whole life to announce what bothers me at the moment that it bothers me rather than bottling it up for eventual explosion! Life, no longer an Elliott Smith song. Imagine that.

It was over oysters and martinis that I told my mother, "I could marry him," and she looked at me aghast, having never heard these words come out of my mouth before. I was thirty-three. When my sister told me, while we were making eggplant Parmesan in a cake pan because I had no real kitchenware yet in San Juan, "Brian would've liked him. He would've thought he was a nerd, but he would've liked him," it was settled in my mind.

—

Ever since the text that brought Israel back to me following my week of aloof behavior, wine has been one of the most significant parts of our shared cultural vernacular. It's a vernacular we continue to build upon and understand each other through: He loves Pinot Noir from Germany; I want minerality and a hint of spice in a skin-contact Semillón from Chile. Though I never had as much of an interest in it as I did in spirits and cocktails, my wine bar stint in the East Village helped me get my bearings with the language, with the pronunciation of various grapes. I'd been to Spain only because of a wine company footing the bill, though I asked them mostly about their sherry brand. (Sherry is fortified wine made in Jerez that can be enjoyed on its own, but it's also a common cocktail ingredient.) He was very into wine, and considering the depths of learning possible as well as the innate pleasure of it, I was down for bottle after bottle after bottle.

Wine conversation was for so long dominated by Europe, by the French, by the mystique, by the certifications... I never thought I could talk about wine the way I easily fell into talking about spirits, which have a more ragtag quality that lends itself to newcomers and wild opinion. They're also pretty stable in terms of flavor. New American gins would have different dominant notes than the juniper of a London dry, but they wouldn't vary too widely: Spirits have very specific jobs in very specific recipes, for very specific moods. There is Beefeater gin at a dive bar; there's also Beefeater gin at a five-star hotel lobby bar. You won't find the same reds and whites being poured at both, though. It's why most folks fall into self-deprecation when asked to describe a wine or what they like in one. I saw it at the bar, where people would throw up their hands and take a guess, not bothering to take offered tastes, because they didn't want to embarrass themselves. It's silliness, but it's also a stand-in for how people think about food broadly: The world of it feels too big and overwhelming, so they default to what's most commonplace or easy. It's not often that we feel allowed space for curiosity or questions in dining—these are luxuries, privileges reserved for those with money and time and inclination. We have to create or find that space for ourselves, and that can take a lot of work and care.

And wine is food, coming as it does from grapes. They tried growing grapes in Puerto Rico, the Spaniards, because they wanted to have communion wine easily available (I'm sure they also wanted wine available for other reasons, too), but the heat created something sickly sweet and undrinkable. Most of the wine available in the archipelago remains Spanish, because of a still-special relationship and the cultural standard that persists that still sees Spanish things as *best*.

So the grapes need to be grown in specific conditions. Despite the Eurocentric nature of wine conversation for many centuries, it originated in Western Asia, or present-day Armenia. Georgia, the country, is credited with the first of what's now referred to as natural wine, a misnomer (as "natural" almost always is) that describes a style of winemaking that is low-intervention, fermented with ambient yeast, often using organically grown grapes—no pesticides. It's bottled with few to no sulfites for preservation, and perhaps aged in qveri, a clay vessel. It's a style of winemaking that has made wine more fun, youthful, approachable—because it's not going by the old rules, it doesn't have to abide by the old hierarchies of knowledge, pairings, and types of places where it's served. Of course, it's become a bit of a joke to talk about, because it's been popular mainly in urban centers among folks who might have been called "hipsters" once upon a time.

But to me, the rising cachet and popularity of natural wine suggests an increase in how much care can be cool when it comes to what we drink *and* eat. Often, natural wine bars or restaurants with menus that stock large quantities of it will adhere to a local, seasonal, or small-batch ethos that complements the wines, which are—yes—perhaps more volatile than conventional bottles but also offer surprising flavors, refreshing effervescence, and the oft-acknowledged "funk" of something like a nice aged cheese or even a bit of cannabis.

Natural wine was always more interesting to me because of this acknowledgment of land, of the fact that it might be more interesting to see what happens in the fermentation of grape juice when it's not messed with for the most precise calibration. Whereas I can find pleasure in interesting distillates (especially those of agave or sugarcane juice), when I am drinking a cocktail on a regular basis, stability and consistency are what I'm after. Wine is different. I like a surprising, messy piece of work, something that jolts me to attention. I want something that reminds me of earth, that reminds me of hands that harvest, not something constrained by a notion of what it should taste like—rather something that asserts itself, guided by a vigneron who knows the land, the fruit.

The wine shop or bar becomes, at least in my closest analogy, the adulthood version of the record store of my youth. I was always a five-foot-tall nerd going into Record Stop in Ronkonkoma and asking some bearded man for something imported from the U.K. or France or some experimental album by guitarists who otherwise spent their time in massive bands. It was why I worked, after all: to get CDs. I would go in with determination. Now I work to get wine—or so it seems. There are worse things to work for. I have come to appreciate different distributors of wine for their taste, too, the way I would've trusted an indie record label or small publisher for their taste. I'll read any book put out by Semiotext(e); I'll drink any wine chosen by José Pastor.

—

The first grape I really enjoyed was a Rotburger from Austria. It might have been because it was the cheapest option where I worked, and thus I felt less bad drinking it at the end of my shifts, but the smoky cherry character of the one we were serving was everything I never knew I wanted in a glass of wine. While I'd always drunk crappy Malbecs or Pinot Noirs, pouring myself a glass at the end of a particularly annoying workday or just getting giddy with friends, this was something new—something distinct. When it got warmer out, I started to prefer a Grüner Veltliner for its gentle effervescence. Because I had to taste all of the wines we served on tap before every shift to know what I was serving, I actually developed my palate a little bit. I could talk a little bit about the wine. We had a Merlot from the North Fork of Long Island that tasted lightly smoky, an interesting character given to the grapes that were harvested around the time of Hurricane Sandy. Channing Daughters, in Bridgehampton, bottled a lovely Ramato, a skin-contact Pinot Grigio. I was learning more about how grapes from Long Island could produce more than sweet swill; I was learning there were people on Long Island who cared about wine the way the farmers I met during my baking year cared about vegetables.

I wasn't confident, per se, but I was getting somewhere. And I still don't really want to "get anywhere" with wine. I want to enjoy it and keep letting it surprise me. Natural wine allows for more of that, even when there's mouse—the hard-to-define flavor of musk that characterizes these bottles, which is really the result of a bacteria that can emerge in any fermented product.

In keeping with how learning about food has let Long Island become a place of beauty rather than the barren wasteland I considered it as a kid, there's a bottle shop in Williston Park that is now part of our routine. There, we marvel at affordable wines that are either not available in San Juan or are much pricier. It's one of those colonial tricks, something that keeps this style of winemaking rarified in people's consciousness—served only with an eighteen-dollar twirl of bucatini in marinara. Back in Patchogue, we indulge: Lambrusco with the pizza from Delfiore that I grew up with; a liter of Milan Nestarec with Szechuan food at my Aunt Diane's house.

The changes on Long Island that have come with care for food, with interest in cocktails, and with—it must be said—a wildly increased cost of living in the city have made for a more robust scene. We visited the two-person team behind Floral Terranes who make stunning local Merlot and Cabernet Franc in a garage. Like my time at the farmers' market and with the re-emergence of local oyster culture, wine has helped me see where I grew up with new eyes. To Israel, it's an exciting place: He wants to see the vineyards, the apple orchards, the historic homes. I can't be grumpy or fall into an easy sullen adolescent mode when I'm back home anymore. He's changed that.

Beyond all the new relationships and understanding it's given me, natural wine has also provided a framework for remembering that we can ferment alcoholic beverages in a way that works with rather than against the environment. While grapes are the standard fruit for winemaking, there has been an emergent movement called Anything But Vinifera, meaning anything but *vitis vinifera*—the common wine grape, the grapes that have come to be synonymous with widely known wines and were brought to the "new world" by colonizers from the old. If wine or co-ferments are able to be made with whatever is abundant and local, on land that is accessible or from fruits that are public, then this changes who is able to make wine and in turn, it becomes more appealing to new drinkers. If wine is no longer synonymous with luxury, but rather pleasure, abundance, and eating from the land, then it can be more open to everyone.

Being open to change is something the wine world has had to be: The effects of climate change have been felt perhaps most acutely by winemakers and grape-growers. It's been a canary in the coal mine for other crops, because of the sensitivity of viticulture and the fact that it's grown in places historically considered very biodiverse. The meanings of grapes, of geographies, will shift and have shifted by necessity. If there is to be wine in the future, the definition of what is luxury will change. The meaning of lands and what they can grow will change: Where once there were grapes, there may be avocados, as has happened in Sicily.

In the Burgundy region of France, famous for its Pinot Noir and Chardonnay, they've been documenting the temperature since 1370. For this reason, it was easy to see when the temperature shot up in 2003 for the hottest year then on record. Most wine is made in the mid-latitude region of the world, in temperate climates—from France over to New York's Finger Lakes and across the States to California—where the summers become hot enough for the grapes to ripen but not so wet that they're subjected to pestilence and disease.

The regions best known for producing large amounts of wine, like Burgundy, the Napa Valley in California, Mendoza, Argentina, regions of Australia and South Africa, and Rioja in Spain and Tuscany in Italy, are most at risk of shifting temperature patterns changing not just the character of their wines but also the ability to grow grapes at all. As regions shift, so will flavor and yield. That famous word *terroir*, which signifies how a crop and a place—its soil, its climatic conditions—come together to produce a unique flavor, is now applied to many drinks and foods, but its origins are in wine.

Everyone has their limits when it comes to new flavors, new bottled funk. Israel doesn't always want to drink the fruit wine that's 50 percent cider, 25 percent rhubarb, and 25 percent currant wines, or a pet-nat the shop owner warns us about for being strange—these things excite me right off the bat, the possibility of some new flavor opening up some new channel in my brain. He's more drawn to convention, tradition. But when I'm told someone is making wine from pawpaw in North Carolina, I feel a thrill: This means the survival of old joys, using ancestral methods, but doing it in new ways. Israel always comes around once we've popped off the metal cap of the bottle. He, too, likes to open up new channels, even if at first he's reluctant.

Conventional wine, in understanding and certifications, relies on very specific practices and flavor profiles. Natural wine and fermented beverages made from other fruits or crops can be less predictable—made of rhubarb, currant, and pawpaw. Letting go of what something is supposed to taste like is the first step toward accepting the potential diversity of flavor that might await a world that no longer values yield and sameness. Wine is where we can see a changing climate up close; wine can be a way of adapting our ways of living and our palates to a brand-new future.

—

It's on the level of the symbolic and imagination that I find the most potential for shifting people's relationship to food and beverage, and thus agriculture and land—and onward toward how we decide value in the first place. Do we let other people decide for us? Do we accept that whatever makes money or can be sold for the highest price is more valuable than something made with care, from the fruits the earth is giving? Fruit here is literal as well as figurative. If using large plots of land to get predictable amounts of grapes (or apples, or cocoa, or wheat) that also taste the same and look the same as the ones we know have come before doesn't really create a world where land, animals, and most people are thriving, then don't we have to change it up? Don't we have to start to value diversity, of flavor, of diet, of how land is used?

When old-school wine writers who know all the conventional wines like the back of their hands start to worry over the emergence of natural wine, what they're really worried about is a change in what is valued. The conventional techniques and flavors are the product of a world where there is a predictable hierarchy of taste, which stems from a predictable hierarchy gastronomically and diplomatically. In this world, the old-school wine writers are comfortable and have thrived. A changing of the guard for them doesn't just mean that they're no longer relevant in terms of their work, but also that the hierarchy to which they've been attached doesn't have the same cachet anymore. They're reactionary against natural wine because it collapses the whole structure upon which the Western world's luxury values are built.

—

This is a lot of work for natural wine as a concept to do, of course. I get carried away, as though I've just had a couple of glasses. It's not perfect; it's not a panacea for the world's ills. There has been worker mistreatment, harassment, and obfuscations about sourcing in this industry as well. It is an industry; it is staffed by human beings, fallible as we are. But the emergence and normalization of a way of winemaking that prioritizes the fruit and the land—that pushes culinary culture toward a more dynamic consideration of value. Shifting palates toward finding pleasure in uniqueness and surprise and even, yes, a little weirdness means possibility. If a grape or a region doesn't have to taste the same every time: What else can that mean for how we eat and drink and enjoy? What else can it mean for how we live? If we're not all elbowing each other to get the best vintage of a Pinot Noir from Burgundy or an Hermès Birkin, does that mean we care more about the effects we have on the planet and each other than what status these things might represent?

Maybe. It's utopian. Though we weren't drinking wine when I said to Israel, "If we're going to get married, we should just get married" (I had a martini, he a Boulevardier made with rye whiskey), the thirty guests at our small Brooklyn wedding were handed a Lebanese pet-nat from the Bekaa Valley rather than the more traditional Champagne. It should go without saying that I baked the cake: chocolate olive oil cake, chocolate ganache, pumpkin-spiced tahini buttercream, with a ring of candied carambola as its topper. To have a good life, I've learned, one doesn't have to shirk all convention—just most of it.

Of course, in becoming a wife, that dreaded word and even more dreaded concept, I was taking on a burden of historic proportions: Could we sustain our own little utopia in marriage? This utopia where those who know us and love us are aware that when we're in charge, the wine will be a little different and the food will be vegetarian and they're probably going to have a vegetable they've never had—or at least not like this; where I'll make the dessert from found fruit or some excess that was dropped off. This is how we try to do things, because it's more interesting to us to live this way. So far, so good on not succumbing to the worst of a power imbalance, even though I'm the one who does the cooking. It's become so ingrained in me to start the day with a consideration of the pantry and what might be going bad, what we need to use, and what we're craving that it only occasionally feels like drudgery; when it does, there's pizza or empanadas to go out for. Israel is the dishwasher, table-setter, and beverage director, a balance that works. We continue to surprise each other; we even surprise ourselves. It's best to be open to changing plans and changing palates. The next bottle of wine might be the one that changes your life.

On Beans

THEY TASTED LIKE SADNESS. THEY WERE THE ONLY THING I didn't like to eat, aside from meatloaf, squishy white bread, and plastic American cheese. White rice and kidney beans on the stove meant a pork chop, a far cry from the fresh earthen flavor of my beloved lamb, and my mom telling me, "*Eat!*" I never usually had to be told. I usually gobbled it all up. But oh, I hated rice and beans. This was another dish that Brian and I agreed on: We didn't want it. Just like when my mom made meatloaf, the memory of rice and beans on the table just feels like a cloudy day. Dull, dour, unmemorable. Except, of course, that I remember these days very well.

You could blame my youthful hate on maybe the beans not being seasoned well enough, but my husband vindicates me when he says he doesn't like the kidney beans, the pink beans, the go-to Puerto Rican habichuelas—he prefers black beans, which are popular in Cuba. Those are the ones I cook every week for tacos and quesadillas, and their rich purple broth is always splashing against the white walls of the kitchen, staining them until I wash it away. But he also doesn't enjoy recao, known elsewhere as culantro, the strong cousin of cilantro, a staple ingredient in the national sauce of sofrito, or even arroz con gandules (pigeon peas), my personal favorite dish of comida criolla, so I don't know how much better I feel because of his cosign.

When I went vegan, I knew that I didn't have a choice anymore. Thankfully, I made that transition in such a wide-eyed stupor and with seemingly boundless energy for learning new things. The ratios for how to cook brown rice? On it! Cooking beans from scratch? I've never done that, but I'd love to soak a sack of chickpeas overnight and then watch them simmer for hours while copyediting with my laptop on the counter. Like baking, vegan savory cooking was a matter of experimentation and knowing where to go for the right answers, whether that was a cookbook or an online recipe. Over time, I became good at making beans.

Now I go on the radio and I say, "Look at the grain and legume traditions of more plant-based cuisines around the world, and start to get a taste for beans that way" with the confidence of someone who knew that all her life. When I told my students on our lunch stop about how pumpkin makes for a good bean broth, using my culinary tidbit to change the subject from colonialism, I didn't include the fact that when I was a child, this dish was my nightmare.

—

Giving up meat required learning how to love beans in all their forms, whether that was simmered simply on the stove to accompany rice, turned into a block of tofu, or fermented into tempeh. Luckily, I had a template in mind for how to figure it out.

The beef pastelillos I'd grown up with provided the perfect way for me to get into the beans I rejected so strongly as a kid. These were empanadas with a flaky, light crust that were usually deep fried. I'd eaten a crab-stuffed one on the beach in Piñones; it would be the last crab I'd eat—but it gave me this idea to just swap the go-to animal proteins for beans.

Instead of beef like my mom or crab like the women in Piñones, I would use those once-dreaded pink kidney beans. They were the only Puerto Rican protein, after all, that I knew to be vegan. I made them from dried, from scratch, adding many shakes of Goya adobo powder to the water as they cooked. The sofrito, a blend of cilantro, culantro, ají dulce, onion, garlic, cooking peppers, and olive oil, would be made from scratch, of course. Once the beans were ready, they'd be heated through and stirred up with the sofrito. My mom had always used the Goya sofrito, the orange Goya frozen shells, but I knew: I needed to make it all myself, so I looked up recipes for the pastelillo dough and adapted it to my ethos, using olive oil as the fat and cornstarch instead of egg. I rolled them out to circles, filled them with the bean mixture and dotted them with briny olives, then closed them with the pressing down of a fork. They were then fried until the outer shell was crisp and bubbly. They came out perfectly on the first try, just like those chocolate-chunk cookies. Even Israel tried one, despite the recao.

The beauty of beans became clear to me by putting them into what had always been my favorite food and making them my way. It was the beginning of an ongoing love affair, an understanding of this really quite diverse legume. Now, multiple times a week, tofu is pressing in my kitchen while my phone is set with multiple alarms reminding me to check the garbanzos on the stove. As with most common ingredients, that diversity had been long obscured by commerce. Supermarkets everywhere and anywhere would have cans and bags of dried beans, but the variety would be minimal: chickpeas, black beans, kidney beans, lima beans... and that was about it. One could be forgiven for not knowing there was far more to it.

—

Beans occupy a strange place in global gastronomy. They're able to grow in most climates, preferring warmer weather and soil temperatures above sixty degrees Fahrenheit. It's estimated that there are more than 400 varieties cultivated around the world. Either we're singing the praises of beans because they have a good relationship with soil bacteria because they convert atmospheric nitrogen into the kind of nitrogen those bacteria like, or we're talking about the ways in which it's a thrifty way to fill up and find protein—or maybe we're talking about soy, a crop that is wildly powerful because of its use as livestock feed that also has the potential to be a protein source for the world.

In his exhaustive book *Eating Puerto Rico: A History of Food, Culture, and Identity*, food historian Cruz Miguel Ortíz Cuadra attempts to explain why the kidney bean, or habichuela rosada or colorada, has become simply the habichuela of Puerto Rican cuisine. He begins by demonstrating how essential to local identity it has become—inextricable, even, especially because the preference for this color sets the archipelago apart from its neighboring nations and their staple black beans.

The indigenous people were the ones who realized beans were good, and grew well among cassava and corn. These were all key to survival under the harsh conditions of Spanish colonization. Enslaved Africans introduced *Vigna unguiculata*, or cowpea, and it too became a staple. Combined with the Spanish taste for chickpeas and lentils, there were legumes on tables in every type of household. But it was the indigenous and African peoples who kept the bean crops alive and thriving. Eventually, it would become common to have two crops of red and white beans per year, in spring and fall, and a winter harvest of gandules, a hot-weather, drought-tolerant crop. The preference for red beans, despite lower yield and their being less disease-resistant than white beans, could be explained by their flavor and volume. They've got more going on. They do the thing beans are supposed to do: fill you up.

—

The habichuelas blancas are the ones I've grown accustomed to finding most locally, whether at the farmers' market or through the app PRoduce, and now I finally understand why: Then and now, they simply grow better under the conditions. Usually they're shelled and frozen, not dried, and cook rather quickly. I asked my friend chef César, who had explained to me why pumpkin could be found in a good batch of habichuelas, what role white beans played in his family meals growing up in Williamsburg, Brooklyn. "For rosadas, they were cooked with tomato sauce, jamón de cocinar, and calabaza," he says. "Blancas we wouldn't add tomato sauce and would add potato and salchichón, the fat farmers' sausage with peppercorns in it." Rosadas were called simply "habichuelas," but white beans were "habichuelas blancas."

"The word 'bean,' like the word 'vegetable,' is indefinite," says a Texas A&M publication called "Our Vegetable Travelers," chronicling how produce has moved around the world. It's linked to from the Food Timeline, which places the origin of "new world beans" at 7000 BCE. I think of "indefinite" here as the more scientific, the more reasonable way to say "infinite." Bean and vegetable are vague stand-ins for a multitude, the way apple served as fruit in ancient times. Basic words that contain all we need to be sustained.

What we know as the common bean, with its Latin name *Phaseolus vulgaris*, originates in the Americas. Europeans would have been familiar with fava beans, chickpeas, and lentils, but not the common bean, of which there are so many types, nor lima beans, which likely originated in Peru. All of these, though, are classified under the scientific family called *Fabaceae.* Indigenous people across the Americas, just as they had in Puerto Rico, knew that beans and corn had a symbiotic growing relationship and, nutritionally, they complemented each other as well. Along with squashes like pumpkin, they comprise the "three sisters": They grow together, and they suit each other in flavor and function.

Despite the infinite possibility of the bean, when I was a child and was responding to them on my plate with despair, I was tapping into a social stigma without really knowing it. Beans have always been considered a food for the poor, food for wartime meat shortages. The gray cloud over my memories of those evenings is the feeling that if we were served beans, something was amiss: We should be on alert for changes, for a cutting-back. That cloud was the fear that there would be beans again the next day, and then the next: Our days of lamb chops and London broil are behind us. What I should have been paying attention to, I'd eventually learn, were the potatoes.

"In any culture where a proportion of people can obtain protein from animal sources," Ken Albala writes in *Beans: A History*, "beans will be reviled as food fit only for peasants." They're not known to be worthwhile in their own right in Eurocentric cultural contexts. If protein from animal sources is available and affordable, it's considered broadly preferable to beans. Even cassoulet, a famous French dish that features Tarbais beans that grow in southwest France, is a meaty dish that also involves pork (in multiple forms), lamb, and duck or goose fat. The beans here are specific and appreciated for their terroir, at least, and hold their own against the deluge of animal flesh.

At the start of the COVID-19 pandemic, sales of beans rose 70 percent and tofu sales went up almost just as much: an assurance against the worst possible future, one without access to refrigeration and ample meat. Within a couple of months, President Donald Trump invoked the Defense Production Act to make sure that wouldn't happen, no matter the cost to workers in meat processing.

—

There has been, over the last decade, a push to make beans more hip. Albala predicted this in his 2007 book. While companies like Rancho Gordo have sold well-sourced, "heirloom" varieties since 2001 and many more have joined them in the years since, it's been more recently that magazines and personalities decided to serve up brothy bowls garnished with charred lemon and fresh herbs, and they're on menus for natural wine bars—fat gigante beans, marinated in vinegar and spices. A little tapa, a bite to help the rosé go down. It's perhaps an overcorrection to the poor reputation of beans as a food of deprivation, as a salve against starvation rather than a satisfying center to a meal. Is there a right way to eat and relate to beans? How do they become desirable without becoming inaccessible?

Because usually once a food is broadly desirable, it

becomes expensive: look at certain kinds of mushrooms or, more appropriately, consider the lobster, as David Foster Wallace suggested in the August 2004 issue of *Gourmet*: The seafloor-trawling crustacean had a reputation as food for the poor and institutionalized until becoming, indeed, gourmet at some point in the 1800s.

Beans, because they're not one ocean-crawling crustacean but hundreds upon hundreds of varieties of a plant, don't really risk the same fate. There will be Goya beans in every supermarket and Rancho Gordo beans in every gourmand's pantry; in my own, they're both equally likely to be found, each for their own purposes. It's the nature of the bean; it's ready to go high and low. This is the truth of a lot of plant foods—see, again, mushrooms—and thus it becomes harder to commodify vegetarian eating as luxurious. That's why it's a hard sell: It's ready-made for a lack of resources, through shelf-stability and ease of preparation. That's why its time is now, and why cooking technique becomes so much more important for imbuing meals with specialness rather than the ingredients themselves doing the heavy lifting (and heavy emissions).

Soybeans, which originated in and are most culinarily significant in East Asia—in Japan, it's known as "the meat of the fields"—have been the ones considered worthy of deep research. That's because it's the most important legume commodity. Not because it's a good, nutritious protein source through tofu, tempeh, or its milk, but because it's grown to feed livestock—the animals who are born and caged to become food. Eighty percent of global soybeans go to feed animals who become protein, with that 20 percent left over becoming food itself. Only a teeny-tiny percentage of soy is grown organically, too: Most is monocropped and genetically modified, requiring a large amount of pesticide and destroying biodiversity in the growing regions. Brazil has overtaken the United States in terms of most soybeans grown, and it's been causing increased deforestation. This is all to feed a taste for meat, a taste for what it means to be affluent, to consume luxury, no matter the cost. Meanwhile, the beans are right there all the time.

—

This consolidation of land for the use of one crop in order to maintain an endless meat supply is not news. Since at least 1971, when Frances Moore Lappé published *Diet for a Small Planet*, she referred to the world's food system as a "protein factory in reverse," in which 80 percent of land provides just 18 percent of calories. Soy is the best example of this because of how absurd it is that it causes so many ecological and social issues when we know how to turn it into so many foods that are ready for human consumption.

It's why soy is so important for the countercultural cuisine movement, from the commune of Tennessee's The Farm to William Shurtleff and Akiko Aoyagi's 1975 *The Book of Tofu*. The latter, in the preface to their *Book of Tempeh*, write they traveled throughout the U.S. in 1976, "hoping to do for soybeans what Johnny Appleseed did for apples," spreading them far and wide. Soy, when grown responsibly, is efficient in terms of water usage and how much protein can be provided. The same complaints they were writing about in the seventies, about how affluent people were eating animal dairy and meat fed by soy rather than the soy itself, are still relevant food system issues. The funny thing is that soybeans are as American as apple pie, even if they don't have as wholesome and easygoing a reputation, because they're used to fuel industrial animal agriculture.

All that land growing soy to feed livestock—how many beans could it grow, soy and otherwise? How many people could it feed if we grew crops together that make sense, for the soil and nutrition, for culture and regionality, as well as delicious meals? Beans have a lot to teach us about efficiency, about interconnectedness. It's important that they're becoming "cool" because it means more farmers are growing them in more regions, capitalizing on that factor by appealing to localized eaters. But it's hard to make a bean bad for the environment. That takes the effort of turning it into a commodity like soy, at the service of agribusiness and industrial animal farming.

—

I don't think much about all of this when I'm cooking a pot of beans, splashing their water onto the wall and making purple stains I'll have to clean up later. It's all so far away from me in my kitchen, but is it? The habichuelas, rosadas and blancas, the gandules in their pods, are growing down the street and on this same land where I stand my feet. I want to think I would've come to love and appreciate beans, would've given up that childhood distaste, without giving up meat. But I wouldn't have, and so I have sympathy for anyone who still considers beans either a special little treat, a fancy heirloom on the pantry shelf, or a food for when you're waiting for payday. Giving up meat forced me to find the luxury in what are to others the foods of survival. This has prepared me for whatever days are to come, and ensured I have a large supply of beans regardless of what's happening in the world.

On Bread

THERE IS A MOMENT IN THE MAKING OF ANY DOUGH when one is reminded of every other dough they've ever kneaded. A flour tortilla rolled out so thin it's almost translucent feels like the shell of a pastelillo or dumpling. A flatbread in process can feel, for a second, like focaccia. The difference between pizza and pita is a level of hydration. Ask a serious bread baker about this and perhaps they'll write me off as an amateur before listing all the nuanced distinctions between these, but if you make breads from scratch, you know: We all feed our similar craving for the softness and satisfaction that flour milled from wheat can provide in different ways, with different stuffings. Every dough begets knowledge that we bring to the next, learning what flour and water are telling us in all their ratios, origins, and iterations.

—

The only bread I saw as a kid was the fluffy white Wonder Bread I would never eat, and loaves of sesame-seeded Italian bread that we ate when we had pasta for dinner. If we hadn't sliced it before putting it in a basket, my parents would rip pieces from it and throw them to each other from either end of the dining room table; whether the throws were lobbed and easy or hard and pointed—this told us the mood they were in for our meal, how fast we should eat our spaghetti.

But I can pinpoint when I first ate bread I liked, bread that made me say, *I get it.* It was from Waldbaum's, the supermarket that was down the block, and it was in a plastic bag with a sticker that read, "Peasant Bread." It was perfectly round and uniformly caramel brown. We sliced it into thin pieces, and it had the taste of yeast. This wasn't good bread, not like we know hearty loaves of fresh sourdough to be now, with their airy crumbs and elegant chew. From my suburban perspective, though, it was finally something decent. It was the equivalent type of experience to when I first tasted Dijon when I'd thought bright yellow French's was all there was to mustard: *I get it now.* I never let myself long for my grandma, but these memories tell me what I might have wanted to talk to her about. Good bread. Good mustard. What else?

—

It was easy for me to give up meat for animals, the planet, biodiversity. What I have struggled with adapting to is the potential future where flour milled from the grain known as wheat is more scarce. I once bought a cup of finely ground flour made from batata, a sweet potato, and failed to make edible crackers. The jar cost twenty dollars. This doesn't allow a lot of room for experimentation. There are traditions of making hearty items with the flours of breadfruit or cassava; I read about how they're making ham-like deli meat out of cassava flour in Cuba, to compensate for meat's scarcity. I see a friend in Colombia, visiting, post a pan de yuca that resembles a sourdough and this intrigues me—I'll have to learn what they're doing. *I'll have to go to Bogotá*, I say to myself, *when I can afford it.*

I find myself aligned with the ranchers and dairy farmers I dislike in this case, the ones who say "that's not meat," "that's not milk" about plant-based products. My internal monologue insists, *That's not bread.* I find that the people who find the most beauty in this potential, who are most enamored of so-called "alternative grains" other than wheat that don't have its high level of easy-working gluten protein, tend to be those who live in temperate climates and wouldn't have to live without such flours, without the snappy crust and airy satisfaction of a good baguette. There are also, of course, those with celiac disease, for whom alternative grains and flours have been a godsend. My desperation isn't about my livelihood, my health, or my identity, the way it is for the ranchers and dairy farmers: It's about fear of what it would mean if wheat were no longer shipped to Puerto Rico, as flour or to be milled. It's also a deeply internalized attachment to Eurocentric gastronomy. One is a problem of potential disaster and scarcity; the other, an issue of imagination that can be easily if not enthusiastically solved.

I had vague notions about ancient grains, like the ones used to make the Ezekiel breads I bought frozen and toasted for breakfast, spread with almond butter. I added spelt to muffins; I played around with amaranth for its crunch; I tried out rye in a chocolate chip cookie, when that was trendy. Like any baker, I had a moment with buckwheat, often grown as a cover crop that keeps weeds and insects away. I was focused more on making sure everything was vegan and tasted good, as well as on using fair-trade sugar, chocolate, and coconut milk and oil. These were where I was most sure of exploitation in the chain, of humans and animals. Using local flour was a no-brainer, but it also was so easy to do in New York. It didn't feel as special as I now know it to be.

It was only in 2009, just four years before I began my bakery project, that Farmer Ground Flour in upstate New York was founded and started to source and mill organic grains grown in the state, including wheat. Though New York isn't an ideal ecosystem for wheat owing to its humid summers, with crop rotation and diverse use of the soil, the movement was the start of an understanding that grains can be a locally sourced food. Historically, because grains can store well, the harvest was something a people could come together for; now, there are farmers who grow everything from rye and corn to oats and buckwheat. Soft wheat for pastry and hard wheat for bread. There's so much grain to grow—why should we stick to one?

"The relative stability of grains, which since ancient times has made them a good food to store," writes Amy Halloran in *The New Bread Basket*, "is the same thing that has allowed this staple to become a commodity, vanishing into the anonymous middle of the country." Grain farmers, millers, bakers, and even folks who are making beer or whiskey have had to make enormous efforts to make grains something that don't fade into the background but are at the forefront of the palate. The very fact that flour doesn't have to disappear, that the white powder we understand as a pantry staple could have a grander expression, continues to be a revelation.

—

Wheat can only withstand temperatures up to seventy-five degrees Fahrenheit. Increased heat and drought, or increased rain—these will compromise production, for the reason they compromise production of many temperate crops: They can only sustain life to a certain point, and pests will thrive upon them in wetter conditions. Wheat, like soy, has a lot of power as a global commodity. Without it, or when it's too expensive, it will be a domino to fall toward calamity. People rely on it for 20 percent of daily calories. Diversifying this dependence, as painful and depressing as it might be in a world where we're accustomed to the crisp crust of a well-made sourdough loaf and a specific fluffy texture in our birthday cakes, is quite obviously a necessity.

Despite this more fashionable recent interest in bread as special, something to appreciate and spend ten dollars on regularly, bread has historically had a connotation of being a basic necessity, an essential means of sustenance, unromantic. It's a way of saying, "I'm for the people," whether that's true or not. Demands for bread are thus part of a salt-of-the-earth vision; bread is about inclusion, feeding everyone. Bread, quite clearly, is not steak. Necessity, not luxury.

In *The Conquest of Bread*, written in 1892, Russian anarchist Peter Kropotkin writes that would-be revolutionaries were too concerned with the high-level questions of what the best way to govern would be rather than how to provide food for the working people. "They discussed various political questions at great length, but forgot to discuss the question of bread," he writes.

—

"Bread and roses" is a political slogan, originating in the women's suffrage movement. It means we have what we need, and beauty, too. During the Arab Spring of the early 2010s, the high cost of bread was a point of protest and a symbol of government failures to provide. "Pan, Tierra, Libertad" is the slogan of the PPD political party in Puerto Rico, and this slogan makes them seem quite left-wing—but they're in favor of the status quo "associated state" relationship to the U.S., not independentistas. They've locked into "bread" as shorthand for care, for an awareness of what working people need, whether that's true in the enactments of their policies or not.

—

Like so many other foods before it, bread has been made over to be "fancy," despite itself, and a subject of mastery and expertise rather than a means of creating food and experiencing the joy of said creation. I make breads—leavened and unleavened—on a regular basis, throughout the week, because I know that to feel full and happy, I need my cabbage salad with a hard-boiled egg snugly wrapped in a flatbread and my summer tomatoes with basil and mozzarella on focaccia, tasting of fragrant olive oil. Now that I'm accustomed to rolling out flour tortillas myself, I can't be bothered with the rubbery ones from the supermarket, and they're the perfect complement to seared mushrooms I've dry-seasoned with adobo powder, smoked paprika, and chili, or black beans spiced with chipotle peppers.

I don't have a sourdough starter because it requires attention that I know, because I've tried, would be antithetical to me actually using it. While I'm good at pantry prepping and meal planning, the ease of having yeast in the freezer to give rise to my breads makes more sense for the flow of my days. I used to be ashamed of this, thinking it made me less of a home cook and less of a food writer. Now, I think, who cares? The best way to do things in the kitchen is the way that enables you to actually cook. I don't need to bake beautiful three-day-process sourdough loaves. I need to eat what I feel like eating.

This doesn't mean baguettes and sourdough loaves aren't on rotation in my kitchen—quite the contrary. (I have one real rule for life, and it's to always have a baguette in the freezer for emergencies.) I've taken to heart the way that baker Rick Easton of Bread & Salt in New Jersey discusses the role of bread bakers in community: When there's a good bread baker around, like my friend Diego San Miguel, support them. It's better to put the money into someone who has the right equipment, the know-how, the hours put in, the access to the best ingredients, rather than seek expertise at home and usually find frustration. Of course, this won't apply to everyone who likes to bake sourdough at home. It does apply to me, who does not.

Living in the tropics makes it obvious that it's better to just pay the bakers. I don't have central air-conditioning to control growth and humidity, not to mention my own comfort. For the same reason I'm not baking cookies in July, I'm not baking sourdough bread at any point in the year when the humidity might leap or drop and change everything about the dough I'm dealing with. I do get a few good days in January, always, when it's time to bake the cookies, when I can do it without cursing because they're falling limp, because they won't stay chilled long enough to form into balls or allow me to cut them into shapes.

I could blame my oven for my lack of home sourdough enthusiasm, which is small and runs on propane gas tanks, but I'm always putting things in the oven, no matter the time of year. People in temperate climates don't seem to understand this. I might not have been able to understand it before I lived it. It's very difficult to intellectually understand relentless heat that only becomes more hot: The relief of winter is not in the lowering of temperatures, but in the reprieve from humidity, a few weeks when the sun simply feels less sharp on the shoulders. When people tell me it's too hot to turn on the oven for the three to four months of their northeastern U.S. summer, I want to know what it would be like to say that from March through October, through November. What would change about me to keep me from my flatbread in August, my focaccia in the thick of hurricane season, my tacos during another day in a week of extreme heat advisories? What normalcy would I be willing to sacrifice to let the heat win? What normalcy will I have to sacrifice eventually?

—

While in New York, making my conscious little choices about sourcing were pricey but easily done; in Puerto Rico, it's taken years for bakers to even be able to access large quantities of well-grown and thoughtfully milled flour—the stuff that's unbleached, with no added preservatives or enriching chemicals. The Spaniards, during colonization, tried to grow wheat (like grapes, like olives) to satisfy their palates, their gastronomic needs. It didn't work, but still wheat was shipped in and a bread culture emerged. There is the basic pan de agua, there are sweet brioche-like Mallorcas, and there's the national bread: pan sobao, made with lard—pig fat—unless it's one of those "cholesterol-free" versions they sell at the supermarket, a nod to concerns about diet-related disease.

Wheat has been described as both local and global: Depending upon where one lives, wheat fields might be part of one's daily landscape. It's also the most traded crop, globally, of all. Thus how it became a grain consumed both where it grows and where it cannot: It's important to diets regardless of its local or imported status. "The love of fine wheat breads is one of the preferences that seems to be universal," writes William Rubel in *Bread: A Global History.* This strikes me, immediately, as a Eurocentric perspective, but wheat is indeed everywhere—the world's dominant grain. How did it happen?

The advent of agriculture in modern-day Iraq around 3,200 BCE saw the emergence of surplus grain (chiefly barley), which led to bread, which led to people who were able to do something other than hunt, gather, and subsist. "What we learn from the literature of Uruk"—believed by archaeologists to be among the world's first cities—writes Rubel, "is that bread was at the centre of their concept of civilization."

This way of using the grain spread to Europe, where it grew well, and the Spanish brought it to their colonies, where, at first, it didn't. Wheat wouldn't grow in the Antilles, of which Puerto Rico is part, because of the tropical climate, but there were drier, cooler regions in Mexico where it did, leading to the enslavement of Indigenous people who preferred their own corn to work the land and the mills. The Portuguese colonizers introduced bread into Japan, and eventually during the time of post–World War II rations, shokupan—Japanese white bread—emerged. In contrast to the colonial introductions, wheat began to be grown in northern China, traditionally home of millet as the go-to grain, about 4,500 years ago when it was able to provide assurance of food during a dry period when millet crops weren't producing as much. There, the grain diversity saved a growing population from hunger, and gave us the wheat noodles and dumplings now associated with the region's cuisine. Wheat there did not have to be used in the image of Western gastronomy.

—

Does everyone just love wheat so much, though, as Rubel suggested? In Mexico, there was a lot of reluctance to adjust the Indigenous people's diet away from corn, and now wheat-based breads and pastries are part of the notion of Mexican cuisine; in Japan, it's been understood as part of a Westernization of the diet, but now the archipelago grows its own specialized varieties. Where it spread by perhaps its own volition, though, it becomes a piece of the cuisine in and of itself, without such baggage. Wheat is a fast-growing, high-yield grain that is endlessly versatile as an ingredient. Chances are good that the whole global population would've been eating it with or without colonialism. But what is done with the wheat, what's expected of it—depending on where you are in the world, there are still those Eurocentric tendencies to tackle. This includes my own preference for baguette over whatever I may one day be able to make with batata: It's neither neutral nor natural, but learned.

A lot of humans' relationship to bread is learned, and not just when it comes to agriculture or milling or baking, but aesthetics and taste. When the bran and germ of the grain are removed, the flour milled from it becomes white. For a long time in history, that extra labor made it more expensive—bread for the rich. Thus, it became desirable. Once it was cheap to make the Wonder Bread I found distasteful as a child, the cachet was gone. I don't know why I personally never wanted to eat fluffy white bread from the supermarket, why I thought sandwiches stuffed with deli meat and cheese were gross, why I made my mom send me to school with chicken legs and green salad or I wouldn't eat. I don't know why, when I finally saw the peasant bread, that I finally understood what bread *should* be. Was it because my earliest days were spent in the company of a woman who labored for my food to make it the best it could be, making me the girl-king, demander of delicious?

—

The white bread of the supermarket—peasant or not—has been built off of a commodity supply chain that leaves everyone vulnerable, regardless of their preferences. Rising temperatures, pests, and drought will continue to disrupt the global wheat trade that we have all become so reliant on, by force or by necessity. The price will go up as the yield goes down. In the same way a taste for bread made from wheat was easily adapted to around the world beyond its origin point in western Asia, there are other grains and root vegetables to grind into flour and regional food diversity to support—sooner rather than later, by necessity rather than taste.

Like the grain growers in New York state, more farmers are focused on how to protect their regional foodways through smart intercropping and increased variety. Grains and beans are grown alternately on farms in Washington state and Oregon, providing local protein that gives back to the soil. There are projects and businesses in Puerto Rico turning plantains, breadfruit, and (yes) batata into flours. Commodity wheat—it's the past, or needs to be thought of that way, before a grain the globe relies on for 20 percent of its calories can no longer be a staple.

If there weren't any wheat coming to Puerto Rico, it would mean that something had gone very wrong with that global supply chain. It would mean that even the high-yield, corporate growers didn't have enough grain to export to the archipelago. We'd have to learn new things—cassava bread, sourdough sans grain. And we'd still be people, regardless of whether these foods would be recognizable in Europe.

But when I chose the peasant bread, was I internalizing class notions, ambient around me, about who ate the supermarket bread with the deli meat? I have no conclusions; I wasn't taking notes in elementary school. But I know now that it was an ambient class-based conversation, like the beans. White bread had begun to be associated with poverty and thus "poor taste" while the gourmands, influenced by that French moment in U.S. gastronomy in the middle of the twentieth century, had been moving toward another style—crusty, yeasty, not sweet. I was always trying to plant my flag among the gourmands, asking to go to fancy restaurants and desiring the pricey pizzas of Delfiore over Rocco's. Our taste in bread tells us about politics, about the cultural world, and it tells us who we want to be in contrast to all the evidence abounding—reams of it, binders full—about who we are. I would dig in my heels, drown myself in debt and denial to be the eater of peasant bread, not Wonder; to be a writer, not locked into an office park on Long Island. This girl-king—she was a brat, with all her entitlement to an interesting and fabulous life.

—

But as Brian taught me, one can neither eat nor write their way away from their own story, their own place, their own origin. Life will chase you down, and losing my brother to an overdose was like having a rope thrown over me that tied me back to the docks of Patchogue. I could never escape it if he couldn't. Learning about the foods of where I came from, from apples to oysters to pumpkin to wines, helped me see it so differently: Could I have helped him see it that way, too? Who would we be now if he'd liked seafood, if he'd known grandma, if he were able to request lamb chops whenever his heart desired? Which breads would we be eating? Once again, I conjure him, put him across from me at this table, the way we sat as children observing our parents, noting how much heft and velocity was in the hunks of seeded Italian loaves they tossed across the table. He tells me nothing, and imagining him alive and happy is almost too much for my heart to bear. I want to know whether he'd be nice about my focaccia or mock me like when I made Mommy the leg of lamb, but I don't get to know whether he'd have grown up.

From Water to Coffee

THE SMELL OF COFFEE WAS SO CENTRAL TO MY CHILDhood that I didn't register it as a smell until I was twelve years old. My birthday had just passed; it was Thanksgiving morning. I woke up not feeling well in a new way: There were no signs of a cold or a stomach virus. Just pain in my abdomen and wooziness in my head. It had all come on suddenly, and when I came downstairs from my room to see my mom in the kitchen, I was hit by what felt like a wall of scent. Deep, dank—coffee. I'd gotten my first menstrual period. My mom gave me a pad and hugged me for so long in the bathroom; I wondered what about this earned me such a lengthy, fierce hug. It was the beginning of womanly vigilance, womanly pain. She knew that, and I hadn't processed it yet. Everything I expected about this moment I'd learned from *Are You There God? It's Me, Margaret*. And they hadn't updated the 1970 writing in 1997, so I didn't know anything.

I'd woken up in that house every day of my life thus far to my mother in the kitchen at the Mr. Coffee but I'd never really smelled it. This still shocks me. What jolted me awake to the scent of coffee? Puberty—becoming a woman, the one my mom would tell not to learn how to cook. When I worked at Starbucks in college, I'd have to be told that I stunk of the stuff. I was constantly rendered nose-blind to coffee, so constant and essential was its wafting presence. Coffee was like water: It was just there, and we all needed it to live. To drink it meant that one was an adult with adult responsibilities that required chemical support to wake up each day—but have I ever really considered coffee a "chemical"? No, it's an elixir, magic. But it's also the only thing I'm chemically dependent upon, and I get terrible headaches if I'm awake for more than two hours without it. I'm going to maintain it's still integral to my life: I will grow my own coffee tree before I give it up, before I admit defeat. Thirst is visceral, whether for water or the satisfaction of an espresso. You can't have one without the other.

—

There was a political flyer in the door of the house where I grew up around an election season one year that announced "Making a Splash for Clean Water in Suffolk County"—a slogan for a state senator, pictured here wearing a pink polo in front of a lake. "Recently, the Suffolk County Subwatersheds Wastewater Plan (SWP) has documented the effects of high levels of nitrogen pollution, not only on the drinking water quality, but on coastal ecosystems," says the other side of the mailer. It had come at an opportune time, when I'd been trying to figure out when it stopped being okay to drink straight from the tap. In the nineties, one day, there were plastic bottles of Poland Spring hauled in from Costco, and those were what we drank. They just seemed to appear like that, and I figured it had something to do with news reports about increased incidences of breast cancer having something to do with the water. I began to see swallowing it straight from the tap as poisonous. I looked up the state senator and found out he's a Republican.

The possible correlation between pollutants in the tap water in Nassau and Suffolk counties, which are the "Long Island" part of the land mass that also includes Queens and Brooklyn, and breast cancer began to be discussed in the early 1990s. Incidences were higher compared to the rest of New York state, and so in 1993, Congress mandated the $30 million Long Island Breast Cancer Study Project. In 2002, the *Journal of the National Cancer Institute* published that the study found no such correlation. So the water was fine the whole time?

Now there are concerns about a chemical found in regular household cleaning products like laundry detergents, which has been found in drinking water. The Yale School of Public Health is looking into this carcinogen called 1,4-dioxane. It is said to be a cause of kidney and liver cancer.

The effect of this is that aside from when I've lived in New York City, where tap water comes in from upstate and its cleanliness is a point of civic pride, I don't drink water straight from the faucet. When people mention the hazards of water in other countries, I wonder if they know about Long Island, about the lead in Flint, Michigan, about the many boil-water advisories in New Orleans, Louisiana, where a combination of old infrastructure, excessively warm temperatures, and testing requirements see residents often warned that they should boil water to remove contaminants before drinking or cooking with it. I wonder if they know that in Old San Juan, I often mindlessly turn on the water, wanting to wash sugar or flour off my hands, to find nothing flowing.

Despite my attempts to get my family onboard with a water filter and reusable bottles, every time I'm in Patchogue, I'm reliant on the same plastic bottles that we got at Costco when I was a kid—and they never actually quench my thirst, so I drink even more. More plastic waste, into the garbage. Or, excuse me, the recycling, that greenwashing bin that helps us not to feel so guilty about all of it.

"What kinds of practical devices, calculations, and arrangements have been deployed to make water into an economic good?" asks Gay Hawkins in *Plastic Water: The Social and Material Life of Bottled Water*. It's a uniquely American phenomenon: The U.S. is the biggest market globally, and between 1993 and 2005, consumption of bottled water doubled, becoming the second largest commercial beverage sold. Hawkins's book characterizes the emergence of bottled water as an "event"—a confluence of invention, health obsession, and privatizing of municipal water systems. That is how it felt to experience the emergence and sudden requirement of having constant water versus just going to the sink or the fountain for a sip: a day-to-day change in our relationship to something ever present. In recent years, different portable cups have come and gone in vogue—a Hydro Flask, the Stanley—creating a new way to overconsume while ostensibly giving up the waste that comes with plastic bottles.

—

As Earth gets hotter, we need more water—consecutively hotter summers in the Caribbean have made that abundantly clear. As Earth gets hotter, water becomes more difficult to obtain. Water scarcity is already happening, beyond just the undrinkable: São Paulo, Brazil, in 2015 and Cape Town, South Africa, in 2018 both came to the precipice of running out. The World Economic Forum has warned of a "water crisis" regularly since 2012; the United Nations notes that "the global climate change crisis is inextricably linked to water." Agriculture uses 70 percent of all fresh water globally, and a third of that goes into meat and dairy. I find myself grinding my teeth as I read about water more than any other subject. Suddenly, a headache. Have I been *hydrating* enough? Better to blame water in the literal sense rather than acknowledge that, in the abstract, its scarcity is what I fear most on a very visceral level. "An estimated 80 percent of the world's population faces high threats to water security," I read. Then, I dry-heave.

There are so many ways to say that it's important to consider the impacts of industrial meat and dairy production, the labor concerns of cacao and sugar, the waterway cleansing capabilities of oysters, the ways in which diversity of apples, beans, mushrooms, bananas, and grapes can demonstrate for us new ways of engaging with notions of desire and luxury that can change our culinary and cultural lives for the better—to bring them into alignment with the earth under our feet. At the end of the day, none of it matters without water, and water isn't to be taken for granted. Water is neither abundant nor is it diverse nor is it a sexy topic that can be dressed up with new recipes or dishes at fancy restaurants: It's simply necessary for everyone, regardless of geography, economics, or what else they like to eat. I dry-heave when I read about water scarcity and drought because I can't be cute about it, the way I can be cute about a bowl of beans or how boring I think it is to be an omnivore. There's nothing left to do but puke.

—

More ink in the food press has been spilled over coffee than water. We can think about how, as a global population, we can "adapt" in the future to a world without coffee because there will be other ways to access caffeine—but to adapt to a world without water? Quite literally impossible. But a world without coffee feels as unfathomable—maybe part of me wanted to live in Puerto Rico so that I could have coffee, chocolate, sugar, and bananas that no one could deny me. All of these are as essential to me as bread, as beans, as wine... perhaps none more so than coffee.

Coffee likely originates in Ethiopia, where the berry was found to have its energizing effects. By the sixteenth century, it was a staple throughout the Middle East, becoming a social drink among Arab populations and arriving in the Caribbean and thus Puerto Rico through the Spaniards in the 1700s. Up in the cooler mountainous regions of the archipelago, Arabica coffee grows beautifully, especially when shaded by cacao and bananas.

Driving up through the mountains of Adjuntas in 2019 was treacherous, and rainfall made climbing the narrow, winding roads even scarier. Visiting the coffee farm known now as Forgotten Forest was one of my first times getting to experience the cool air of the tropics, when you're so high up that it feels like you're among the clouds. The coffee here is handpicked from the bushes where the berries grow green and turn their ready red. We toast fresh beans on a stovetop and drink the pour-over while our guide opens up a cacao pod and shows us its pulp and seeds. This is the first time I meet chocolate in its original state, plucked right from the tree. My friend Ricky, who was photographing the farm, and I both had tears in our eyes: It was his first time, too, and he'd grown up here.

At this farm, they're growing small-batch beans for a specialty market. While coffee had for over a century been a big business for Puerto Rico, there are now only 4,737 farms, compared to the 21,693 farms that had been registered and exporting in 1899. The local beans had supposedly been the preferred brew of the Vatican for a time in the twentieth century—the favorite of the pope!

Now there is no export business, and a lot of the coffee marked "Puerto Rican" at supermarkets and branded with old names like Café Rico is owned by Coca-Cola. Their local company is called Puerto Rico Coffee Roaster, and it owns 80 percent of the production, yet uses only a small percentage of local beans; the rest will be green coffee imported from other countries and then mixed in. It is akin to how the once robust but exploitative sugar industry now imports the raw material, as do the larger rum brands. All the things Puerto Rico, under Spanish colonialism, was known for are shells of their former selves, being restored in small, artisanal pockets. What could be built now or in a future free Puerto Rico is something altogether new, untethered to the needs and demands of colonizers.

—

But the archipelago faces so many challenges from the weather. A tropical storm, Ernesto, in August of 2024 caused $23 million in loss from crops—chief among them, plantains, bananas, and coffee. Even farmers who intercrop plantains and coffee to ensure they are more resilient to strong winds lost their plantings to landslides caused by torrential rain. Water gives, water takes. From 2014 to 2016, the archipelago faced such extreme drought that restrictions were put on usage, but there has increasingly been this back and forth between downpours and drought. Neither extreme is good; neither extreme sustains a farmer long enough, well enough. And Ernesto wasn't called a hurricane, which hurts their chances of recouping damages with insurance companies.

While hurricanes and storms have their own very terrifying effects, it's the notion of drought that makes me most fearful of the future, of the disasters that are wrought by climate change. I'm a person of islands; I'm accustomed to large bodies of water. I'm accustomed to the shortening of the shore over time by erosion, too. Coffee crops are in more danger from lack of water than they are by increasing heat—indeed, it's the main environmental stressor affecting yields. There are studies done to see how we can grow coffee under drought conditions, which cover crops and compost work best to mitigate arid air and soil. Water is necessary not just to brewing but to growing coffee—perhaps it's the clearest through line from source to café.

Globally, there are already those who are living under conditions of what's called water stress, where lack of available water meets insufficient water cleaning and moving infrastructure. Southern and Central Asia, as well as North Africa, are currently the most water stressed regions in the world. But drought is being experienced everywhere from the Amazon rain forest, Pacific Northwest, Zimbabwe, Spain, Greece, Moldova, Romania, and Mexico. West Virginia, in 2024, has reported drought conditions for the first time in the history of monitoring. It's so widespread that it feels absurd to name where it's happening, but the effects of climate change tend to be discussed most openly when they're affecting poorer nations or the global south. Just like naming the places in the U.S. where drinking water from the tap isn't always advisable, it's important to note the prevalence of water scarcity as a human problem that is creeping up on everyone.

—

Water and coffee have been taken for granted: turn on the faucet, water. Wake up in the morning, coffee. Perhaps it's a bag of beans hand-harvested in the hills of Ciales, Puerto Rico, and gently ground in a burr before being brewed in a Chemex. Often, the origins are not so explicit even if *the coffee always comes from somewhere* (like the chocolate, like the sugar, like all of it). That was my mental response while I read a Patti Smith book, *Year of the Monkey*. She was longing for a mug of coffee that tasted like nowhere, without terroir or named origin. Diner coffee in a thick white mug, poured by a career waitress who's snapping gum and calling you "honey." I don't blame her: It's the American promise, abundance from nowhere touched by no one's hands. In San Juan, we are blessed to begin each day outside in the Plaza de Armas with our espresso from the kiosk of Cuatro Estaciones, where we see neighbors and Benny our dog is served a large biscotti container filled with icy water. We start our day this way, the way so many people in the world do—espresso, a moment of calm before the storm of work and responsibility. Caffeine might make adult life and productivity under capitalism possible, but it also makes for moments of slow serenity and spontaneous community. Rituals have purpose; we just have to own their narratives and our time.

By 2050, experts say, a bulk of the best coffee-growing land on the planet will be incapable of growing the most popular variety, arabica. Does this mean Adjuntas? Does it mean Ciales? There are "solutions"—the ever-present notion of "adapting" to the loss of everything we've ever known to constitute our daily lives and pleasures; there are technological advances—anything we can do to keep our coffee. I sympathize with this. I don't want to lose my coffee either, as I don't want to lose my baguettes. There are limits to work-arounds—we can't change anything about how humans are causing climate change and its destruction; humans are buying endless amounts of plastic and ignoring that everything they have has come from somewhere. For how long will the adaptations suffice? As with the erosion of the shores, we end up somewhere in the dunes, beating back the waves of an ocean strengthened by human hubris and warmed by human indifference. At that point, there's nothing to eat, nothing to drink.

I'm afraid of the future, and so I'm going to get up and cook, because that's how I've learned to show up to the world. Despite knowing that the world is heating, it's one way to exert control. The choices in how we source ingredients, approach our precious resources like water and coffee, and consider how to share the joy that is always attainable through food and gathering around a table will always matter. Indeed, the after-dinner cup of espresso might change someone's thinking, and then another's, and another's, until there's a groundswell and we realize the changes necessary to curtail the potentially enormous loss that is at our doorstep. Trying, believing—in the process, at the stove, there's joy.

—

When I brought my cousin Richie to the New York City vegetarian restaurant Superiority Burger and the chef dropped a mixing bowl on our table of fresh nectarines sliced and sprinkled with sugar, I felt the power of my special relationship with food. It was my first time in their new space, which had taken over a classic New York diner on Avenue A, right across from Tompkins Square Park, and they had not changed all that much about the look aside from the art on the walls. The tables had paper placemats that advertised local East Village businesses, and the pastry case was stocked with cakes just like the diners I grew up going to, where chocolate mousse was what I clamored for. I'd already been emotional about the fact that this vegetarian diner was packed: It felt like my youth was meeting my adulthood; the child I was meeting the woman I'd become; and maybe the world was ready for a life less meaty. The fruit dusted with sugar was, even before I took a bite, taking this entire experience over the top. Then I picked up a piece of nectarine and ate it, turning teary-eyed to my younger cousin, who was across the table: "This is weird," I said to him, "but if you'd met our grandmother, she would have fed you this."

Having had a few glasses of wine, I nearly shoved the fork in his mouth myself: I never got to really share my grandma with my cousins, and this moment was truly Proustian. While my mom, aunts, and uncles all got something different from her and all tell different stories, my relationship to her, as short as it was, was simple. She showed she loved me by feeding me, often lavishly; she showed me that lavish could be as nonchalant as good fruit sprinkled with sugar. Usually, these were strawberries—hulled and sliced, the sugar extracting their juice and taming any tartness. I have the sense the chef knew what he was doing when he put that on our table, that I could love good fruit—or, not just love, but be enraptured by it, without pretensions. My love of food doesn't come from an impossible pursuit of mastery or a taste for only the finest things: It comes from childlike delight, and it comes from my grandma. It comes from knowing that a little bit of sugar mends the failures of out-of-season strawberries. A lot has changed since my Long Island youth as the girl-king, eater of lamb chops and lobster. But it's always her joy that I serve.

—

I did not heed my mother's warning: I became the woman who cooks, who bakes, and who writes about all of it—where the food comes from, the fact that it was touched by human hands or was a sentient being, the possibility that we may not have quite as interesting a culinary future as we have had a past as a species. I've become both a professional and a domestic worker. Do we hear about a woman who cooks any other way? Julia Child, Ina Garten—the one I watched with my grandma and the one who would later remind me of her. They've invited audiences into their homes and made it look easy. Our diets have changed more in the last 150 years than in the million years that preceded, and women have been at the helm of making it palatable, beautiful, and nutritious. Domestic labor and the performance of its perfection is part and parcel of the suburban domesticity so integral to the American Dream. The angel in the house, who makes it all happen with a smile.

Like Child and Garten, I'm married but without children. This seems an ideal perch from which to preach the tenets of a good food life: We have someone to perform for on a daily basis out of care and not as wage labor, but we're not so burdened that we can't leisurely pop into the specialty grocer or have a phone call with our baker friends. And we're women, so there's the sense that we are happy to give freely of our knowledge.

I think about my grandma, who cooked for five children and then me, and my mom, who cooked for us every day after work. Both of them didn't let food feel like duty, drudgery, though no one would have blamed them for doing so. My mom would cart us around to all different grocery stores on Long Island looking for things she'd heard about on TV, like bulgur wheat. Was it a way to stay close to my grandma, like the rosemary she put on the roasted potatoes? Why didn't she want me to feel the same way about food, ever in search of something new? Why did I end up doing it anyway: shucking oysters in Scotland and getting food poisoning in France? Seeking mushrooms in the tropics and finding my way home?

It was my move to the city, I think, and my reconnection to Puerto Rico, that allowed me to free myself finally from a fate I didn't want. Even though all of my grandparents had moved out to Long Island in the hope of a better life, suburbia proved a trap. It didn't fix the addictions of my paternal aunt and uncle. It was where my brother began to use drugs and ultimately died from that addiction. My grandma, without a license, was stuck and used food as her way to travel and be creative. The soil might be fertile—might produce stunning apples, pumpkins, and grapes—and its waters might be home to some of the world's best oysters, but there is poison in the taps.

—

Food set me free in that way I'd always dreamed of being: not a domestic snare, but the seed of the life I'd always wanted. I don't want to perform perfection, so I don't; I want to reveal the messiness of trying to do one's best to tread lightly, how nearly impossible that is as an American but how that doesn't make it not worth trying, worth caring about, worth investing in. We can change our desires, reconsider our luxuries. I am pessimistic about the future, but I am deeply committed to the present, to making each day and every meal count: delicious, beautiful, and done with care. But not in the way women have been trained to do, forced to do: as an act of resistance to powerful forces that want to see humanity fed one boring, destructive, corporate diet. Diversity, care—these are weapons we can wield. The food in our pantries and on our plates is within the realm of our control.

There is no way to divorce my early appetite for lamb chops and chocolates from the fear I feel for effects of a warming world, warming ocean, on how humans and animals and plants will continue to live and survive. I've tried to make sense of these appetites for so long now. I've tried to make them fit into boxes—vegan, vegetarian, fair trade—and still, I am going to puke when I think about drought. I was given one appetite and I've remade it, and in doing so, I remade my own life.

Do I care about the fate of Earth because of any altruistic urge, or is it another sense of grief—the planet itself slipping away from me the way I lost my grandma and my brother? How much more can I lose, can you lose, before we've got nothing left that we either need or enjoy—no water to quench our thirst, no coffee to converse over, no oysters to slurp and martinis to sip? What world are we leaving for the next girl-kings? What appetites are we cultivating?

Altruistic or narcissistic or just a symptom of anxiety—it doesn't actually matter why one cares, why one adjusts. It only matters that we do. The care can begin in the kitchen, as mine did, against all my resistance to being a woman tied up in apron strings, or it can begin in the fields or at the market or in the grocery store or the bookstore. If I never got obsessed with food, with baking, and became vegan, even if I'm vegetarian now, would I be a writer at all? Would I be married to my husband? There was a domino effect from my grandma's lamb chops to coconut oil butter chocolate chip cookies to piña coladas and back to oysters that led me to this life. And now, onward. To the next meal.

Acknowledgments

A few months into writing the first draft of this book, I had a migraine. I'd never had one before. It came on like a regular headache and subsided a bit when I found a pair of silver Dries Van Noten heels on sale, but then ramped up toward dinnertime. It was a windy, raining, cold March Saturday and my mother's sixty-first birthday. The pain dissipated once I vomited, which I read online is common. Rather than celebrate, we spent the evening on the couch, and I had my head on my mom's shoulder. It reminded me of my brother's head on my shoulder. I'd just written the chapters about oysters and martinis. The migraine was unrelieved grief and stress.

Which is all to say, I have a lot of Alanis Morissette "Thank U"–type feelings about the experience of writing this book, and I have to first say thank you to the migraine for letting me in on what was happening a little bit deeper down than I wanted to go. Thank you to my editor, Renee Sedliar, for being with me every step of the way and getting it so fully. I couldn't have written this with anyone else. Thank you to my agent, Jenny Stephens, for having always gotten it and being my more discerning eyes.

To Kerry Roeder, Doug Bleggi, Candice Carr (always your name to me), Luke Schordine, Justin Teague, Kylie Blohm: I love you and thank you for being around during the darkest and lightest times. Thank you to Layla Schlack, Mayukh Sen, Charlotte Druckman, and César Perez for being my food media comrades.

To my mom, Leslie, thank you for the food, the books, the magazines, and being you. To my sister, Cameron—Brian and I weren't excited about you coming along, but I have no clue how I'd live without you. To my dad, for the music and drives on Ocean Parkway.

Thank you to my husband, Israel Meléndez Ayala, for the inspiration and the martinis and the laughter. Thank you—last but never least—to Benny, my daily companion and the dog I always wanted.

Bibliography

Ken Albala, *Beans: A History* (Bloomsbury Academic, 2017).

April Bloomfield with J. J. Goode, *A Girl and Her Pig* (Ecco, 2012).

Rosalind Coward, *Female Desires: How They Are Sought, Bought and Packaged* (Grove Press, 1985).

"Nothing can be as local as what emerges from the terroir of a single self," wrote Charlotte Druckman,

Lauren Elkin, *Art Monsters: Unruly Bodies in Feminist Art* (Farrar, Straus & Giroux, 2023).

M.F.K. Fisher in a 1975 *Esquire* piece titled "Apple Pie."

Andrea Gentl, *Cooking with Mushrooms* (Artisan, 2022).

Amy Halloran, *The New Bread Basket* (Chelsea Green Publishing, 2015).

Gabrielle Hamilton, *Blood, Bones, and Butter* (Random House, 2012).

Gay Hawkins, *Plastic Water: The Social and Material Life of Bottled Water* (MIT Press, 2015).

Anissa Helou in *Saveur* in 2009.

Erika Janik, *Apple: A Global History* (Reaktion Books, 2011).

Madeleine Kamman, *When French Women Cook* (Clarkson Potter, 2010).

Thomas Keller, *Ad Hoc at Home* (Artisan, 2009).

The Conquest of Bread, written in 1892 by Russian anarchist Peter Kropotkin.

Nigella Lawson, *How to Eat: The Pleasures and Principles of Good Food* (Houghton Mifflin Harcourt, 2007).

Eugene Stock McCartney, "How the Apple Became the Token of

Love," *Transactions and Proceedings of the American Philological Association* 56 (1925), 70–81.

Sidney W. Mintz, *Sweetness and Power: The Place of Sugar in Modern History* (Penguin Books, 1986, reprint).

Sidney W. Mintz, *Worker in the Cane: A Puerto Rican Life History* (W. W. Norton, 1974, reprint).

Frances Moore Lappé, *Diet for a Small Planet* (Ballantine Books, 2021).

Jenny Offill, *Dept. of Speculation* (Knopf, 2014).

Cruz Miguel Ortíz Cuadra, *Eating Puerto Rico: A History of Food, Culture, and Identity* (University of North Carolina Press, 2013).

David Rosengarten with Joel Dean and Giorgio DeLuca, *The Dean & DeLuca Cookbook* (Random House, 1996).

William Rubel, *Bread: A Global History* (Reaktion Books, 2011).

Michael Ruhlman, *Ratio* (Scribner, 2010).

Laura Shapiro, essay "Do Women Like to Cook?"

Laura Shapiro, *Perfection Salad: Women and Cooking at the Turn of the Century* (University of California Press, 2008).

William Shurtleff and Akiko Aoyagi, *The Book of Tempeh* (CreateSpace, 2014).

William Shurtleff and Akiko Aoyagi, *The Book of Tofu* (Ballantine Books, 1987).

Patti Smith, *Year of the Monkey* (Vintage, 2020).

Texas A&M publication called "Our Vegetable Travelers."

José Trías Monge, *Puerto Rico: The Trials of the Oldest Colony in the World* (Yale University Press, 1997).

Virginia Woolf, 1931 speech, "Professions for Women."

RAISING READERS

Books Build Bright Futures

Thank you for reading this book and for being a reader of books in general. We are so grateful to share being part of a community of readers with you, and we hope you will join us in passing our love of books on to the next generation of readers.

Did you know that reading for enjoyment is the single biggest predictor of a child's future happiness and success?

More than family circumstances, parents' educational background, or income, reading impacts a child's future academic performance, emotional well-being, communication skills, economic security, ambition, and happiness.

Studies show that kids reading for enjoyment in the US is in rapid decline:

- In 2012, 53% of 9-year-olds read almost every day. Just 10 years later, in 2022, the number had fallen to 39%.
- In 2012, 27% of 13-year-olds read for fun daily. By 2023, that number was just 14%.

Together, we can commit to **Raising Readers** and change this trend. How?

- Read to children in your life daily.
- Model reading as a fun activity.
- Reduce screen time.
- Start a family, school, or community book club.
- Visit bookstores and libraries regularly.
- Listen to audiobooks.
- Read the book before you see the movie.
- Encourage your child to read aloud to a pet or stuffed animal.
- Give books as gifts.
- Donate books to families and communities in need.

BOB1217

Books build bright futures, and **Raising Readers** is our shared responsibility.

For more information, visit **JoinRaisingReaders.com**

Sources: National Endowment for the Arts, National Assessment of Educational Progress, WorldBookDay.com, Nielsen BookData's 2023 "Understanding the Children's Book Consumer"